PUDDLES and WINGS and GRAPEVINE SWINGS

Things to Make and Do with Nature's Treasures

for kids and their grown-up friends

A KIDS' STUFF BOOK

illustrated by Gayle Seaberg Harvey

by
Imogene Forte and Marjorie Frank

We wish to thank you, Dana Baer, for countless hours of editing, titling, encouraging and fixing. We're surely glad you stuck with us through this project!

ISBN 0-86530-004-6   Library of Congress Catalog Card Number: 81-85014

Can you keep a secret?? Then follow me
Through meadows and woods to the open sea,
Through craggy cracks in city walks,
Through fields of scraggly, huskery stalks.
Run with me through seasons' doors
And sneak through chinks in cabin floors,
Fly up and away to starlight skies,
Slide back on shadows just your size;
And then . . . . . then you'll begin to see
The secret . . . . . . Shhh . . . . . . 'tween you and me . . . .
That the best, most beautiful, greatest stuff
Of which there's NEVER not enough,
Comes from Nature's lovely store;
Her shelves are filled with fun galore!
And except for things like paste or glue,
An occasional jar or worn-out shoe,
Perhaps some soap or snips of string,
You needn't have another thing—
'Cuz the lady who paints the days' sunrises
Has a zillion more surprises . . . . . .
. . . So leave your paper and pencil chores
And follow me to the great outdoors!

*This book is dedicated to the kids in our lives who
love to splash and tromp in puddles
track down winged and creeping creatures endlessly
and will swing on anything that hangs!*

*. . . and to the kids in ourselves . . . who join
them often in splashing and chasing and swinging.*

Table Of Contents

HURRAH FOR THINGS THAT GROW!

HURRAH FOR DAYTIME & NIGHTTIME SKIES!

HURRAH FOR THINGS THAT CREEP & CRAWL & SWIM & FLY!

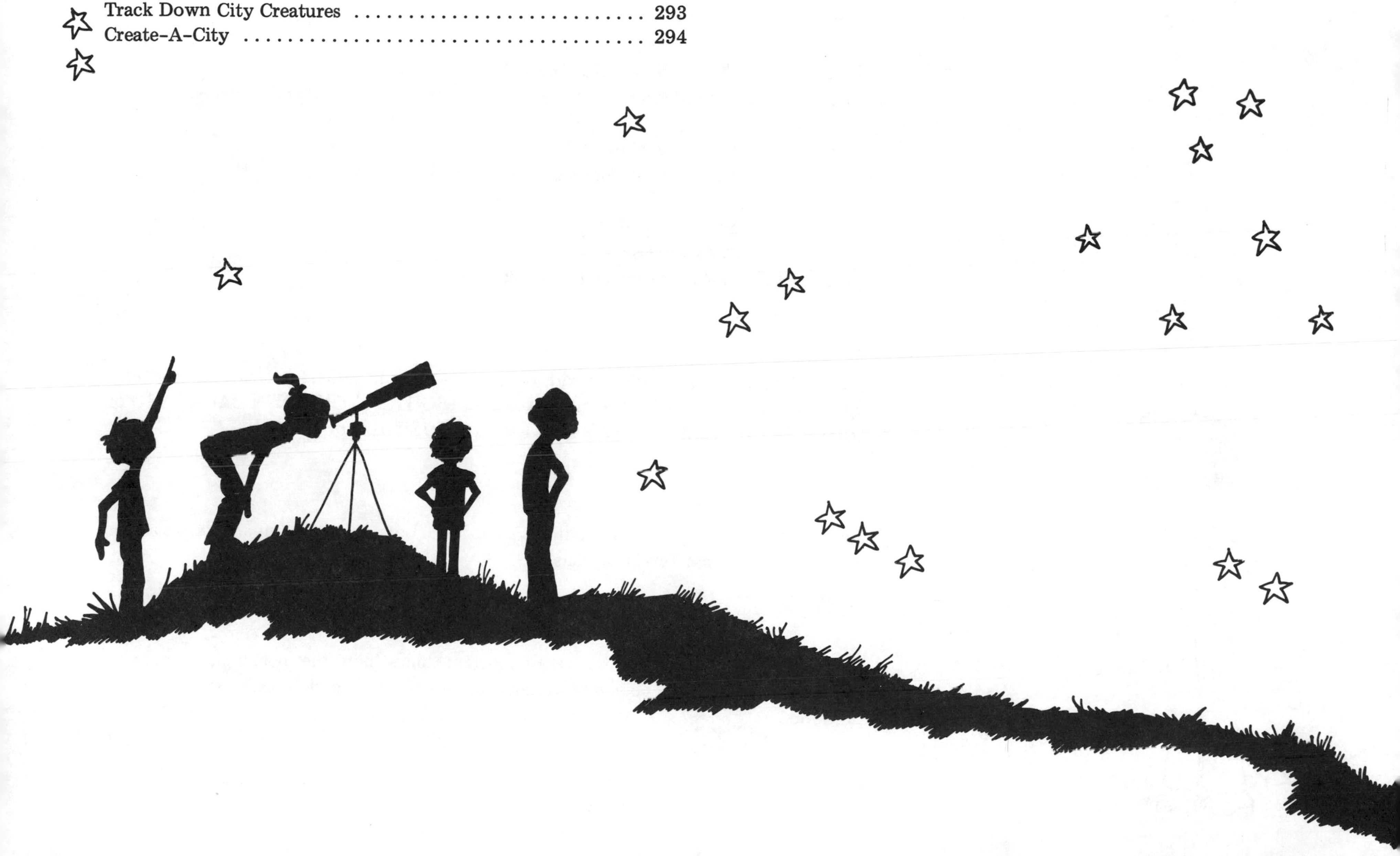

A Letter To Kids

Dear Kids,

HURRAH FOR THE GREAT OUTDOORS!
It supplies you with all kinds of chances for wonderful adventures and projects!

There are . . . places to explore!
    . . . good materials for creating crafts and gifts and works of art!
    . . . wide open spaces for games and trips!
    . . . things to grow!
    . . . animals to visit!
    . . . things to watch and touch and hear and try!

You can explore and experiment with nature's treasures in parks, forests or on beaches. But best of all—you can have nature adventures RIGHT IN YOUR OWN BACKYARD or DRIVEWAY or ALLEY—or on YOUR FRONT SIDEWALK or PORCH!

And yes, you can even bring the outdoors INSIDE! Lots of indoor fun and games and crafts can be started with natural materials.

What's more—you can learn some very important things about the special places and treasures that nature provides—while you're having fun. You can learn how to take care of the great outdoors!

This book is called *Puddles and Wings and Grapevine Swings*. That's because it has such exciting adventures as

> playing and snooping and painting in mud puddles
> getting to know things with wings
> finding or making your own outdoor swing.

There's much, much more, too. Just look at the book's contents on pages 4–7 to see what else this book has in store for you.

The folks who wrote this book want you to enjoy using it. Here are some of our suggestions that will make the book fun and easy to use:

* Before you do an activity, read the page or pages all the way through. You'll notice that every activity has a **What to Use** and a **What to Do** part. Gather all the stuff on the **What to Use** list; then begin with Number 1 on the **What to Do** directions.

* Look at pages 12 and 13. These pages will give you ideas of good things to keep on hand for the activities in this book and for other nature activities. You might want to start your collection right away.

* You'll find that pages 14 and 15 suggest some ways to save and share and show off the things you make or collect outdoors.

* Before you begin ANY of the activities, read the RULES FOR ENJOYING NATURE'S TREASURES on pages 10 and 11. It is important that you follow these rules whenever you use outdoor spaces or materials.

Most of all, we hope you have a great time adventuring and creating with natural stuff!

Rules For Enjoying Nature's Treasures

Nature's treasures are all the things you see around you that are not made by humans . . . air, water, ground, seeds, animals of all kinds, trees and flowers and other plants and people—including YOU. EVERYONE needs to learn to take care of these treasures. So learn these rules and remember them whenever you're using and enjoying the outdoors.

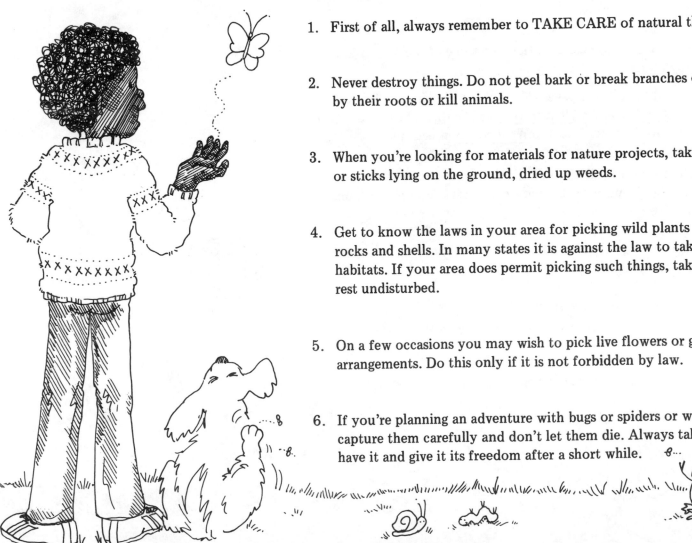

1. First of all, always remember to TAKE CARE of natural things.

2. Never destroy things. Do not peel bark or break branches off living trees, or pull up plants by their roots or kill animals.

3. When you're looking for materials for nature projects, take only fallen leaves, branches or sticks lying on the ground, dried up weeds.

4. Get to know the laws in your area for picking wild plants and flowers or for picking up rocks and shells. In many states it is against the law to take these things from their natural habitats. If your area does permit picking such things, take just a very few and leave the rest undisturbed.

5. On a few occasions you may wish to pick live flowers or grasses for drying or making arrangements. Do this only if it is not forbidden by law.

6. If you're planning an adventure with bugs or spiders or worms or frogs or other animals, capture them carefully and don't let them die. Always take care of the animal while you have it and give it its freedom after a short while.

7. Learn how to enjoy nature's treasures without using them up. Take pictures of things often. Identify plants and animals, watch natural happenings, ask questions, study books about outdoor life and ecology. All these things can be done without interfering with natural processes.

8. For your own safety—NEVER, EVER eat or taste plants or berries you find and DO NOT touch animals unless you are very sure they're safe.

9. When you go off exploring, do these three things for your own safety:

   * get permission from the adult in charge
   * tell someone where you are going and how long you plan to be gone
   * take someone along with you

10. ALWAYS clean up after you've done an outdoor activity. Don't leave trash or footprints or junk scattered around. Do not go into a natural place and rearrange it by moving rocks or logs or things around. Try to have this as your motto:

    "When I leave a space, no one will be able to tell that I was ever there!"

Good Stuff To Gather

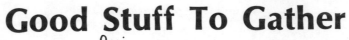

It's not too early to start gathering good stuff for nature crafts and adventures. Start with natural things, then look for other odds and ends that might come in handy. You'll also need some general supplies for making and doing as well as a few tools for games and trips and investigations and gardening. Here are some suggestions of thing to round up!

NATURAL STUFF

dead leaves	seeds	interesting rocks and pebbles
nuts	weeds	bark from fallen trees
dried up flowers	sand	pine cones
sticks	stones	shells
fossils	gourds	feathers
grasses	seed pods	deserted bird's nest

OTHER GOOD STUFF TO HAVE AROUND

jars	bottles	corks
milk cartons	straws	aluminum pie pans
clothespins	cotton	rope
egg cartons	paper bags (all sizes)	old clothes and hats
plastic bags	innertubes	boxes (all shapes and sizes)
old tire	fabric scraps	wallpaper scraps
spools	buttons	nails (not very sharp or rusty)
plastic bottles	cardboard tubes	wood scraps
tin cans	old sheets	scraps of lace and ribbon
newspaper	old toys	old pillowcases
rags	mirror	plastic containers
flower pots	bottle caps	scrapbooks

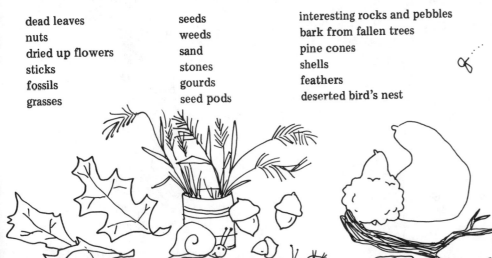

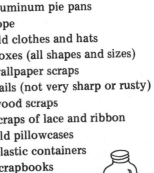

BASIC KIT FOR CREATING

paper of all kinds and colors
cardboard
pens, pencils, markers, crayons
paint and brushes
scissors
paste or glue
stapler and staples
yarn or string
plaster of Paris
lots and lots of newspaper

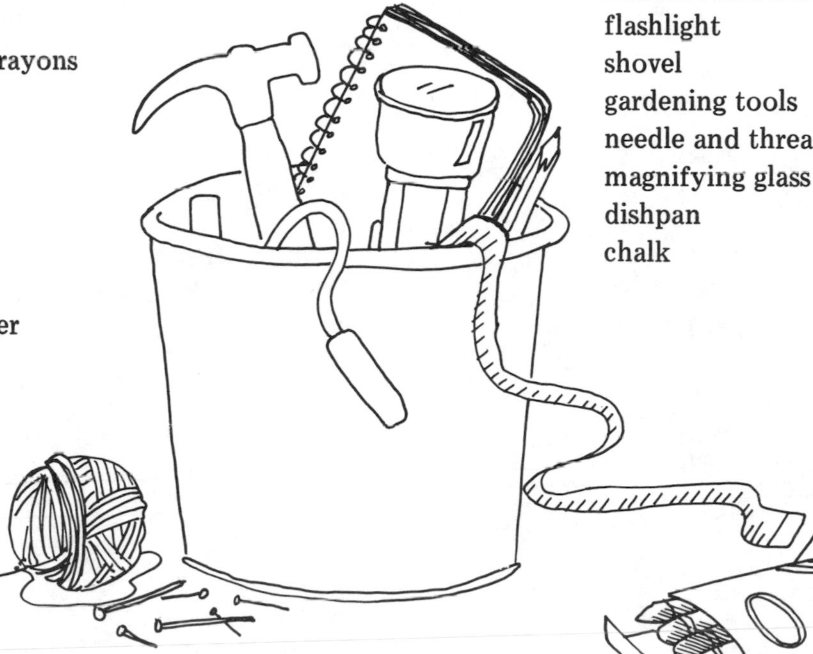

TOOLS FOR ADVENTURING and EXPERIMENTING

hammer and nails
flashlight
shovel
gardening tools
needle and thread
magnifying glass
dishpan
chalk

notebook and pencils
utensils for cooking
directional compass
jump rope
long ropes
exercise mat
measuring tape
measuring sticks

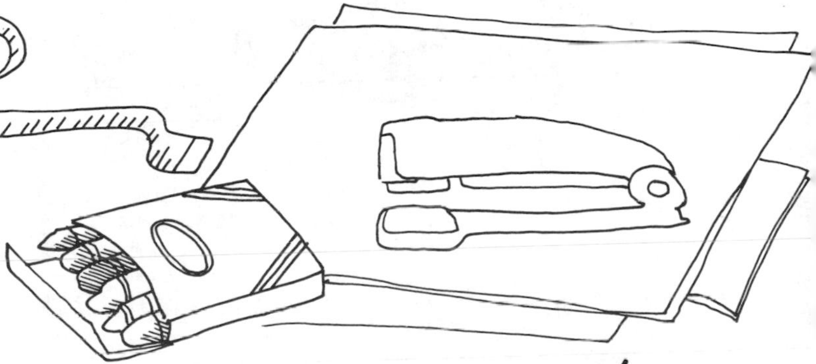

HOW TO KEEP and ORGANIZE YOUR SUPPLIES

Sort your good stuff and store it in containers.

cereal boxes
pails
cans
baskets
bags

shoe boxes
dishpans
plastic containers
milk cartons (tops cut off)
boxes

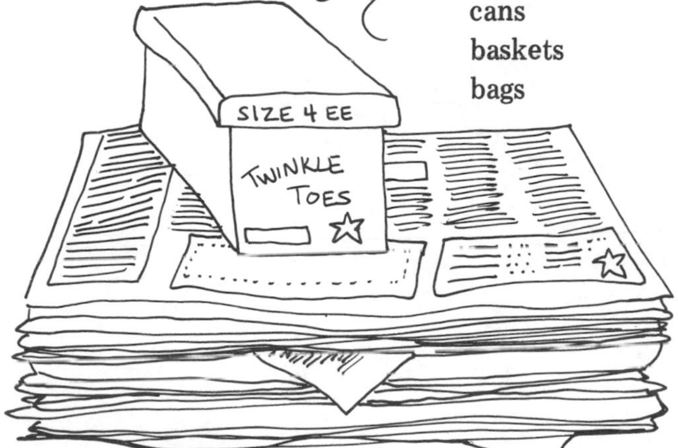

SIZE 4 EE
TWINKLE TOES ☆

13

Save & Share & Show Off Your Collections

Show off special rocks or shells or leaves or seeds or weeds or bark or pebbles in a DO-IT-YOURSELF SHOWCASE.

* Glue fabric on the inside (bottom and sides) of a shallow box. Cut dividing pieces from sturdy cardboard, cover them with fabric and glue or staple them into place. (The illustration shows how to cut the dividers longer than needed to form tabs for gluing.)

* Arrange your treasures in the showcase. You may need a dab of glue to hold each one in place.

* Hang the showcase in your room or any other spot where it will get plenty of attention!

Make a SCRAPBOOK for saving and sharing dried leaves, leaf prints or rubbings, dried flowers or seed designs. Start with a loose-leaf notebook. Decorate the cover. Then carefully glue your special items on pages of heavy paper. Cover any of the very delicate things with clean adhesive-backed paper.

Keep an OUTDOOR LOG for photographs, notes, weather charts, outdoor autographs, inventories and the other interesting records you collect of things you do or find outside.

Use cereal boxes to create FILE BOXES for your NATURE MAGAZINES.
Cut away the top and one narrow side of the box (as shown).
Cover the box with colored paper and decorate it with leaves or other natural items.
Protect the whole file box by covering it with clear adhesive-backed paper.

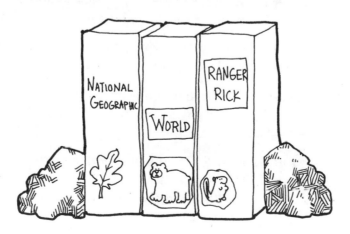

SOME WORDS TO GROWNUPS

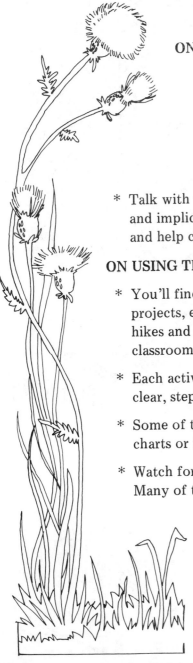

ON KIDS & NATURE . . .

* The very best role you can play is one of SHARING NATURE WITH CHILDREN. Go outside with them. Explore. Notice. Ask them questions. Point out things. Help them collect. Time you spend helping them appreciate the variety, the beauty, the wonder and the fragility of their environment will be LEARNING and GROWING time of great value in their lives and yours.

* Talk with them seriously about the RULES FOR ENJOYING NATURE'S TREASURES. Discuss the meanings and implications and practical applications of these ideas. Learn the environmental protection laws in your area and help children understand and follow them.

ON USING THIS BOOK . . .

* You'll find literally hundreds of challenging experiences in *Puddles and Wings and Grapevine Swings* . . . crafts projects, ecology activities, holiday gifts and decorations, gardening help for young folks, experiments, recipes, hikes and trips, games, investigations. We believe that the pages of this book will fill many needs in your classroom, home, camping or summer school, or church school or scout programs.

* Each activity supplies a list of materials to be used so that you can gather these ahead of time. You'll also find clear, step-by-step directions for all experiences.

* Some of the pages are marked with a ✦. This means that you have our permission to copy those recipes or charts or inventory sheets in a number necessary for the kids with whom you're working.

* Watch for opportunities to combine the activities with learning units in science or math or social studies. Many of them complement these content areas beautifully.

* At the end of the book is a list of books you'll want to consult for nature activities and environmental awareness.

* THIS BOOK IS NOT JUST FOR KIDS! It's for grownups and families, too. Try to DO these activities WITH your kids as often as possible! They'll be good for you and the kids!

Hurrah For
Sticks
& Stones!

Put Your Nose to the Ground

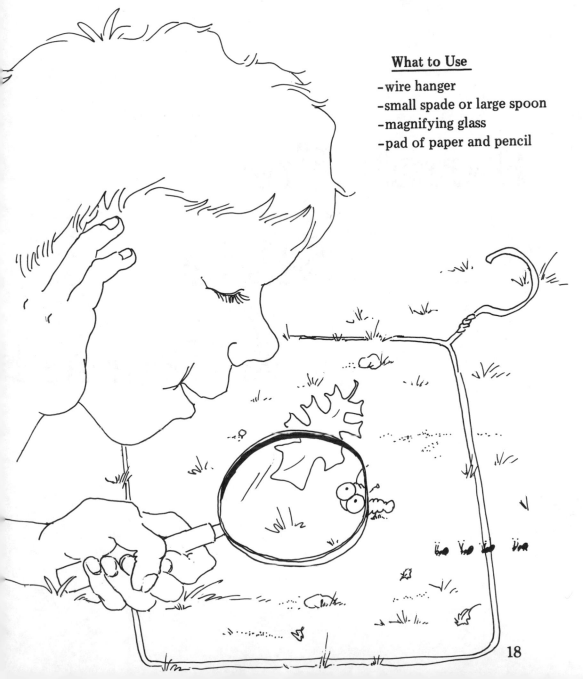

What to Use

- wire hanger
- small spade or large spoon
- magnifying glass
- pad of paper and pencil

What to Do

1. Find a spot of ground to investigate. Make sure that this is in a place where people won't mind if you do a little digging.

2. Bend the hanger so that it is nearly square. Lay this on the ground.

3. Now you are going to try to find out everything you possibly can about that square foot of ground. Start by using a magnifying glass to look closely at the top of the soil. Write down everything you see (grasses, loose dirt, decaying leaves, weeds, pebbles, insects, etc.).

4. Next, dig very carefully into the soil. As you dig, notice the layers in the soil.
   —Draw a diagram of the soil layers.
   —Make a list of everything you find in the soil. (Use the magnifying glass.)
   —Write a description of the soil. (Is it wet? dry? sandy? rocky? clay?)

5. Repeat the investigation in a totally different location and compare your results.

6. After each investigation, carefully return the soil to its original place.

Have A Ground Parfait

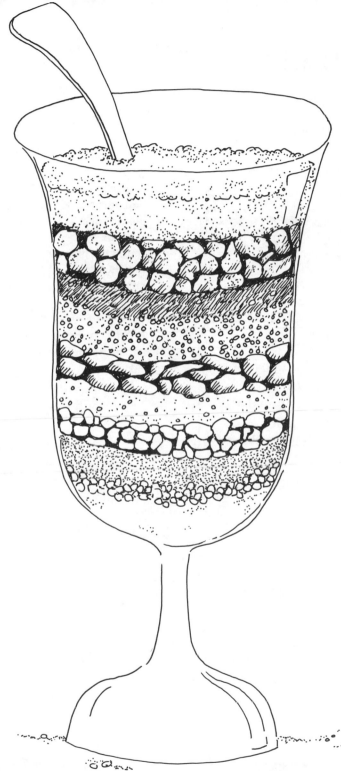

What to Use

- sand of various colors
- fine dirt
- gravel
- small pebbles
- other textures and kinds of dirt
- containers for the dirt and stone
- funnel (You can make a paper funnel.)
- tall glass container
- large spoon

What to Do

1. Use the containers to collect various kinds, colors and textures of dirt and stones and sand and gravel.

2. Choose one kind for the bottom layer. Spoon it into the funnel until the jar has a layer of about an inch.

3. Continue pouring more layers, each time using a different kind of "ground." Make the layers different thicknesses. Try to vary the colors as you build your parfait.

4. Set your finished parfait somewhere that will be a good spot for showing it off OR give it to someone for a gift.

CAUTION: Make sure no one eats it!!

MUD PIES and other delicacies

There are many marvelous concoctions you can stir up with ingredients you'll find outdoors!
You can serve them to your dolls or have pretend banquets with your friends.
Here are a few recipes to get you started. Just gather your materials and start mixing!!
Just be sure that no one really eats these concoctions!

What to Use

– tools such as:
  - egg cartons
  - empty milk cartons
  - orange juice cans
  - pop bottle caps
  - plastic cups
  - shoebox
  - tinfoil pie pans
  - muffin tins
  - cupcake papers
  - cookie cutters
  - sticks for stirring
  - spoons

– ingredients such as:
  - dirt
  - water
  - pine needles
  - flowers
  - weeds
  - grasses
  - pebbles and gravel
  - sand
  - leaves

DANDELION DIP

Stir water into a cup of dirt until you have a creamy mix. Add a dash of sand for flavor.

Dip freshly picked dandelions into this mix for a tasty appetizer.

MUDBLOSSOM LAYER PIE

Pour a layer of mud into the bottom of a pie tin. Arrange a layer of flower petals on top. Repeat with another layer of mud and another layer of petals. Top with a sprinkling of minced weeds. Bake in the sun two hours.

STONE SOUP

Place two rocks in a large milk carton. Add water and set on a hot rock or sidewalk to simmer in the sun. Add bits of grass and bark and gravel for a hearty flavor. Season with a pinch of dirt. Spoon the soup into egg carton sections and serve.

"SAND"WICHES

Make a smooth mixture of mud and fine sand. Spread this lightly on pieces of bark, flat leaves, or between two thin, flat rocks. Enjoy your sandwich with iced rain tea.

GRAVEL MUFFINS

Mix equal parts of gravel, dirt, and water. Slowly stir in a handful of crushed pine needles. Put a heaping spoonful into each section of a muffin tin. Bake on a hot rock all day. Serve with cloverbutter.

ICED RAIN TEA

Place a bowl or pitcher outside during a heavy rain. When you've caught enough rainwater, add a few sprigs of mint and serve over ice.

SUMMER SALAD

Toss together lightly: leaves
                                     weeds
                                     dandelions
                                     grasses
                                     daisies
Top with a dressing of water mixed with seeds.

Can you create a recipe for pine needle tea or a dirtberry shake or moss souffle or mudpuddle mousse or stir-fried worms or sand casserole or roll-out mud cookies?

CLOVERBUTTER

Break up several pieces of clover. Stir these into a smooth mud mixture. Spread the butter on muffins or breads or sandwiches.

ROUND MUDLOAF

Fill a mixing bowl half full of fine dirt. Toss in some snipped grass and a half cup of sawdust. Mix well. Slowly pour in water and mix until you have a thick gooey batter. Press batter into a round tin or a jello mold. Bake in the sun until firm.

SAND! terrific SAND!!

Oh! How much you can do with sand!!
Here are just a few sand adventures.

What to Use

- sand (from a sandbox, hardware store, beach, or sandlot)
- digging tools: paper cups
  - sticks
  - spoons and shovels
  - pails
- white glue
- food coloring
- pencils and cardboard
- small jars
- crayons
- small toy vehicles
- cornstarch
- water

PAINT SAND DESIGNS

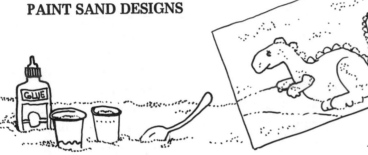

1. Plan a design by drawing with pencil on the cardboard.

2. Color the sand by dropping a few drops of food coloring into a cup of sand. Stir well and let dry.

3. Decide which area you want to cover with the first color of sand. Spread glue all over this area.

4. With a spoon, shake the sand thoroughly over the glued area. Wait five minutes and shake off the excess sand.

5. Repeat the process with the other colors.

PLAN A HIGHWAY SYSTEM

1. Use shovels and spoons to create a network of streets and roads and highways in your sandbox. Don't forget to level spots for parking lots, turn-arounds, rest areas, fuel stations, exit ramps, and toll booths.

2. Use cardboard and crayons to make signs and signals. Poke sticks in the signs for poles. Plant the signs in the proper places.

3. Use your sandbox highways for your small toy cars and other vehicles.

BUILD CITIES OR CASTLES OR FORTS OR HOUSES

1. Clear a flat place on the ground, beach, or sandbox.

2. Mix some water into your sand to get it slightly damp.

3. Map out the outline of your construction project.

4. Use your hands and sticks and shovels to pile up walls.

5. Pack sand into cups and other containers to make towers and turrets and steeples and roofs. Gently shake these out by turning the container upside down.

6. Add roads and signs and gates and windows by drawing in the sand with sticks and forks.

7. Enjoy your sand creation quickly. Often these crumble because the sand dries out or mischievous visitors come by!

MAKE A SAND SCULPTURE

1. Mix 2 C sand
   1 C water
   1 C cornstarch

2. Heat and stir until the mixture gets thick.
   Ask an adult to help you with the cooking.

3. When the mixture is cool, use your hands to mold it into an interesting shape. Poke and punch and squeeze to create noses and eyes and designs.

4. Let the sculpture set until it is dry.

Layered Sand Planter

What to Do

1. Get some sand from the beach or hardware store. If possible, try to collect different natural textures and shades of sand or several pastel colors of chalk may be pulverized and added to portions of the sand. A layer or two of fine gravel or very small shells may be used to add interest.

2. Fill the container by layering the sand in a pleasing combination of textures and colors.

What to Use

- several colors and textures of sand
- round glass container with wide mouth (some pickle jars are perfect for this)
- tin can
- charcoal
- soil
- philodendron, ivy, or other vine house plant

3. Remove both ends from the tin can to make a tube. Push the tin can tube into the center of the sand in the container. Scoop out the sand that comes into the tube. (Make sure the top of the tube is below the top layer of sand.)

4. Drop several small pieces of charcoal into the bottom; then fill the tube with soil. Add the plant and water it thoroughly.

24

Shell Silhouettes

What to Do

1. Arrange your shells on the cardboard in an interesting design.

2. Draw lightly around each shell with the pencil.

3. Remove the shells and squeeze white glue along the shell outlines.

4. Use the spoon to drop sand onto the glued surfaces. Use plenty of sand and allow the glue to dry before you shake the extra off.

5. If you like your handiwork, you can give it a coat of clear shellac to make it last longer. Then mount it on heavy brown paper. If you think it's <u>really</u> special, you may want to frame it under glass.

What to Use

- flat shells
- pencil
- sand
- white glue
- cardboard or heavy white paper
- large spoon
- clear shellac
- brush

Shell Belt

What to Do

1. Try to find two fan-shaped shells with holes in them. Or you can use tree bark instead, but make sure you find it on the ground or a dead tree.

2. Wrap the rug yarn around your waist and tie it, then add ten more inches to it. Cut two pieces of yarn that length.

What to Use

– shells or bark
– feathers
– rug yarn
– scissors
– white glue

3. Twist the rug yarn to make a cord. Pull each end of the cord through the holes in the shells or bark. Knot the cord so that the shells or bark won't fall off.

4. Arrange the feathers on the shells or bark and glue them in place.

A Fine Feather Pen

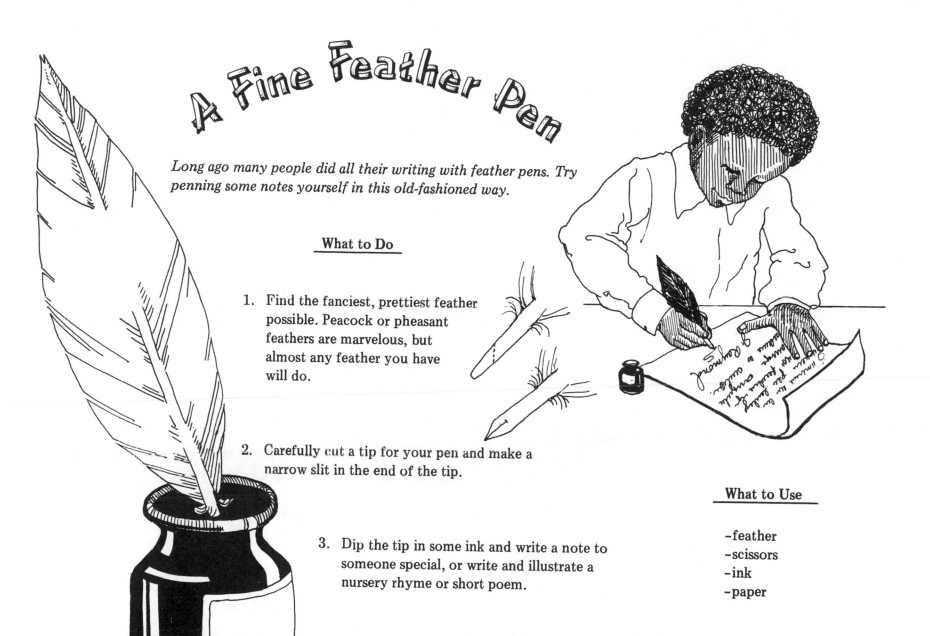

Long ago many people did all their writing with feather pens. Try penning some notes yourself in this old-fashioned way.

What to Do

1. Find the fanciest, prettiest feather possible. Peacock or pheasant feathers are marvelous, but almost any feather you have will do.

2. Carefully cut a tip for your pen and make a narrow slit in the end of the tip.

3. Dip the tip in some ink and write a note to someone special, or write and illustrate a nursery rhyme or short poem.

What to Use

-feather
-scissors
-ink
-paper

GOURDS GALORE!

What to Use

- long-handled gourd
- knife
- water and soap powder
- enamel in the color of
  your choice
- small paint brush
- clear shellac
- leather thong or cord
- potting soil
- ivy or other vine plant

What to Do

1. Cut a hole in the front of the gourd to form a bowl.

2. Scoop out the pulp and seeds; then wash and dry the inside of the gourd. (Dry the seeds, too, and save them to make seed pictures!)

3. Paint designs on the outside of the gourd and allow to dry.

4. Cover the entire surface with clear shellac and let it dry overnight.

5. Make two holes in the top of the gourd and run the cord through to make a hook for hanging.

6. Fill the bowl with soil and plant your vine.

To provide a home for a very small bird, follow the same directions through step 5. Omit the soil and plant. Instead, put some straw inside to make the lucky bird comfy. Hang the bird house from a post or shrub in your backyard, and wait for a tenant!

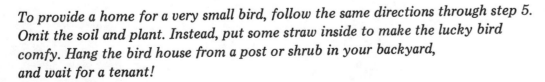

28

Hang A Gourd

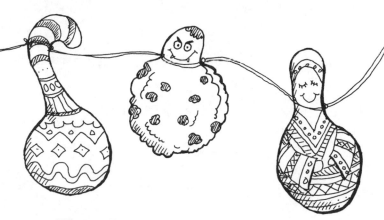

What to Use

- gourds
- dishwashing detergent
- paper towels
- enamel or poster paint
- small paint brushes
- clear shellac
- rope or string

What to Do

1. Select firm gourds with interesting shapes.

2. Wash the gourds in water with a little dishwashing liquid in it; then dry the gourds thoroughly.

3. Use different sizes of paint brushes and colors of paint to make designs on your gourds.

4. Allow the painted gourds to dry completely and then paint them with a coat of clear shellac.

5. Use rope or string to hang gourds for kitchen or patio decorations.

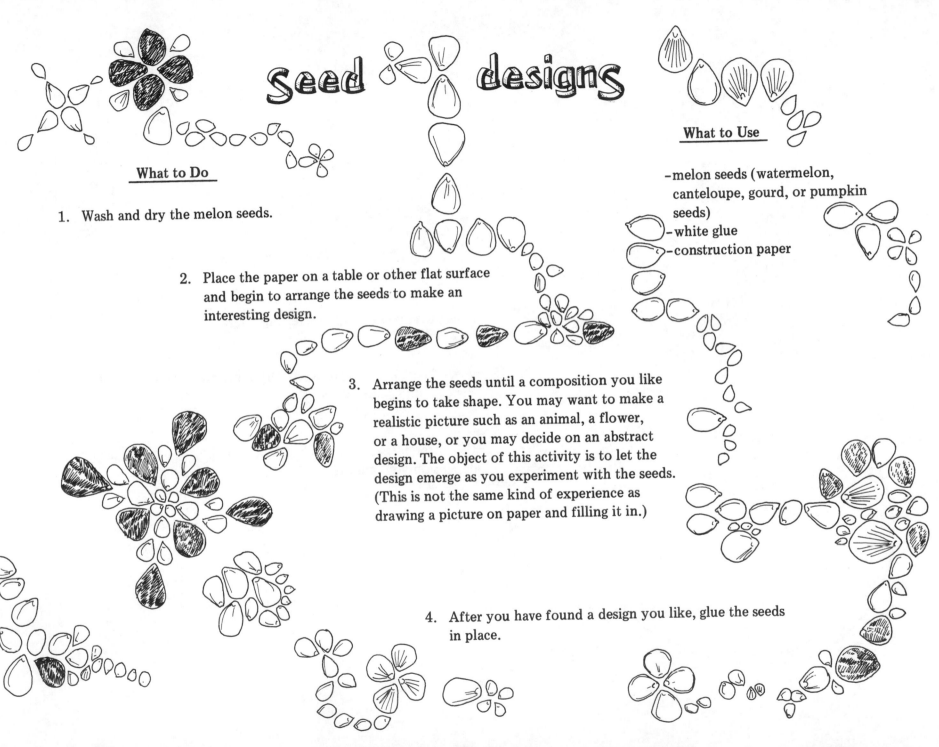

Seed designs

What to Use

- melon seeds (watermelon, canteloupe, gourd, or pumpkin seeds)
- white glue
- construction paper

What to Do

1. Wash and dry the melon seeds.

2. Place the paper on a table or other flat surface and begin to arrange the seeds to make an interesting design.

3. Arrange the seeds until a composition you like begins to take shape. You may want to make a realistic picture such as an animal, a flower, or a house, or you may decide on an abstract design. The object of this activity is to let the design emerge as you experiment with the seeds. (This is not the same kind of experience as drawing a picture on paper and filling it in.)

4. After you have found a design you like, glue the seeds in place.

30

Pebble Portraits

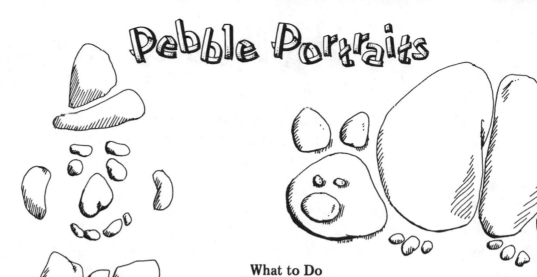

What to Use

- small pebbles
- box top (shoe box works well) or
- heavy cardboard
- white glue
- pencil

What to Do

1. Collect small pebbles of different sizes, shapes, and colors.

2. Spread the pebbles out in the box top so that you can choose the right ones for certain spots.

3. Use the pencil to outline a portrait of a person or animal on the cardboard. (You might like to make a king, a witch, your pet, a make-believe creature, or even a self-portrait!)

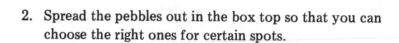

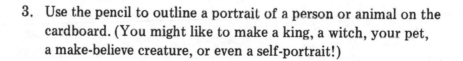

4. Arrange the pebbles to form the portrait. Use many shapes and sizes and look for special pebbles for the eyes, nose, etc., to give interest to your portrait. When the arrangement suits your fancy, glue the pebbles in place.

Try cars, buildings, flowers and other creations!

for the love of a rock

Everybody needs to have one rock that is his or her very special, favorite rock. Here's how to choose a rock to be your friend. Take lots of time to find just the right rock for you.

What to Use

- your sharpest eyes
- a sensitive mood
- plenty of time
- a spot where there are rocks

2. As you are looking for the right rock, follow these rules:
   - *Your rock should be big enough to keep from getting lost in a drawer.*
   - *Your rock should be small enough to fit in your hand.*
   - *It should have just the RIGHT feel on your skin.*
   - *The rock should look good from ALL directions.*
   - *It should smell good to you.*
   - *It should look good all by itself, away from the other rocks.*
   - *It should look good when it's wet.*

What to Do

1. Head for a place where there are plenty of rocks. It is a good idea to go alone, so you won't be hurried or distracted.

3. Carry your rock around with you for many days. Feel it and smell it and look at it often.
   - *Can you draw its portrait from the side and top and bottom? Try it!*
   - *If you put it in a basket with many other rocks, could you find yours again? Try it!*

32

Rocky Personalities

Collect small rocks from a lake, an ocean, or a mountain stream site. If you can't get to any of these places, just look along the sidewalk or roadside for smooth rocks with unusual shapes. When you have several to work with, you'll be ready to begin your "Rocky Personalities" creations.

What to Use

- rocks
- poster paints
- paint brush
- liquid wax or clear shellac
- newspapers

What to Do

1. Cover your work surface with newspapers.

2. Select one rock at a time. Look carefully at it before you start to paint. Often, the shape and texture of the rock will give you ideas for what to make with it.

3. Paint the face or body of a person or animal on the rock. Or paint flowers, landscapes, or abstract art. Let your imagination run wild!

4. Coat the finished creations with liquid wax or clear shellac.

5. These make lovely paperweights or desk decorations, and are good souvenirs of a vacation trip.

Stone Gnome

- all kinds of stones
- soap
- water
- pan for washing
- glue
- waxed paper
- paints
- brushes
- clear shellac

*Some people think that gnomes grow from stones under the earth!
Whether or not this is true, you can make your own gnome out of stone!*

What to Do

1. Look through your collection of stones and choose a large one for the body and two smaller, flat ones for feet and one for the head. Try to find a stone that looks like a craggy face to add personality to your gnome.

2. Wash the stones carefully and let them dry.

3. Cover your work surface with waxed paper.

4. Put the two flat feet stones on the waxed paper and drop some glue on them.

5. Wait a few minutes and then place the body stone in the glue on top of the feet stones. Allow the glue to dry thoroughly.

6. Drop some glue on the body stone and let it sit for a minute or two. Then put the head in place and allow the glue to dry.

7. Use your paints and brushes to give your gnome features, clothing, and personality. (You may use scraps of paper and cloth, too.)

8. Allow your painted gnome to dry and then cover your creation with clear shellac. Let the shellac dry overnight.

Spicy Forest in a Jar

In just a matter of minutes you can put together a pretty spicy forest in a jar to make your favorite kitchen smell too good to leave!

Mmmm!

What to Do

1. Wash and dry the jar.

2. Spread a mixture of allspice and ground cloves an inch thick in the bottom of the jar.

3. Create a forest scene using a whole cinnamon stick for bark, whole cloves for flowers, dried grasses and straw flowers for interest, etc. Add pebbles or tiny animals for decoration.

4. Tie a ribbon and a small bunch of straw flowers around the top of the jar.

5. Give your spice forest in a jar to your favorite cook with a note telling him to remove the top and leave the jar open for a few minutes when the air in the kitchen needs a bit of spicing up!

What to Use

- small jar with a top (Use the prettiest one you can find around the house. Sometimes the ones vitamins or bubble bath come in are just right.)
- allspice
- ground cloves
- cinnamon sticks
- whole cloves
- dried straw flowers
- dried grasses
- tiny animal figurines (if you have them)
- tiny pebbles or rocks

This is specially for you. Open it up when you need some'pi' good smellin'. Love Kandi

35

Rocky Top Box

-small, sturdy gift box
-stones, rocks, and pebbles
-liquid white glue
-material
-scissors
-ruler

3. Wash and dry the stones and rocks. Be sure to polish them with a soft cloth so they will shine as much as possible.

4. Arrange the stones in a pattern that you like to fit the top of the box. Glue them into place one at a time (let each drop of glue dry a little before you press the stone onto the box top). Set the box aside to dry overnight. In the morning, your "Rocky Top" keepsake box will be ready to fill with treasures.

What to Do

1. Choose a small sturdy gift box with a top.

2. Measure the inside sides and bottom. Cut material to fit and glue it into the box.

36

Nature Banner

What to Do

1. Cut a strip of burlap and fringe one end of it.

2. Fold the other end over the tree branch, and use the needle and thread to stitch it in place.

3. Cut a narrow strip of burlap to use for the hanger. Fringe both sides and the ends of the strip. Tie the fringed strip to each end of the tree branch to form a hanging loop.

4. Arrange your natural materials on the burlap. Glue or sew in place (some of the things such as twigs, bark, etc., may be too heavy to be held by glue, while flowers and leaves will be best glued).

What to Use

- burlap
- sturdy dead tree branch
- white glue
- needle and thread
- natural materials (shells, twigs, tree root pieces, feathers, bark, dried flowers, pressed leaves, fossil rocks, etc.)

37

Weathered Wood Wall Hangings

What to Do

1. Search for unusual and interesting shapes of weathered wood. (If the desired piece is not as aged as you would like, you can make it more interesting by beating it with a hammer and/or scratching it with sandpaper or nails.)

2. Keep the shape and texture of the wood in mind as you gather the natural materials to be used for decorations.

What to Use

- old barn wood, fallen tree bark, driftwood, or firewood scraps
- glue
- decorative natural materials like dried straw flowers, twigs, empty insect nests, nuts, seeds and seed pods, feathers, grasses, etc.
- picture hanger (available at hardware or variety stores)
- hammer, nails
- sandpaper

3. Place the natural materials on the wood until you have an arrangement that pleases you. Then glue the materials to the wood.

4. Attach the picture hanger to the back of the completed wall hanging.

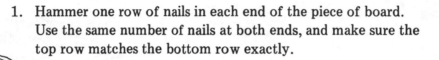

Outdoor Weavings

What to Do

1. Hammer one row of nails in each end of the piece of board. Use the same number of nails at both ends, and make sure the top row matches the bottom row exactly.

2. Take a long piece of sturdy string or yarn. Tie one end of it to the first nail on the bottom. Loop the string up and around the first nail at the top. Then bring it back down to the second nail at the bottom and up to the second nail at the top. Keep looping the string back and forth until you have reached the last nail at the top. Keep the string tight as you work.

3. Tie the string to the last nail and cut off the extra.

4. Take a piece of grass or weed. Weave it over the first string, under the second, over the third and so on. Weave the second item under the first and over the second. Always weave the feather or weed or grass OPPOSITE from the one above it.

5. Use a variety of colors and sizes of items to make the weaving interesting. You can add some bits of colored yarn if you'd like.

6. When your loom is full, attach a piece of yarn to the top end nails to make a hanger for the weaving.

What to Use

- heavy string or yarn
- nails and hammer
- board (not too thick)
- grasses, weeds, dried flowers, feathers
- yarn
- scissors

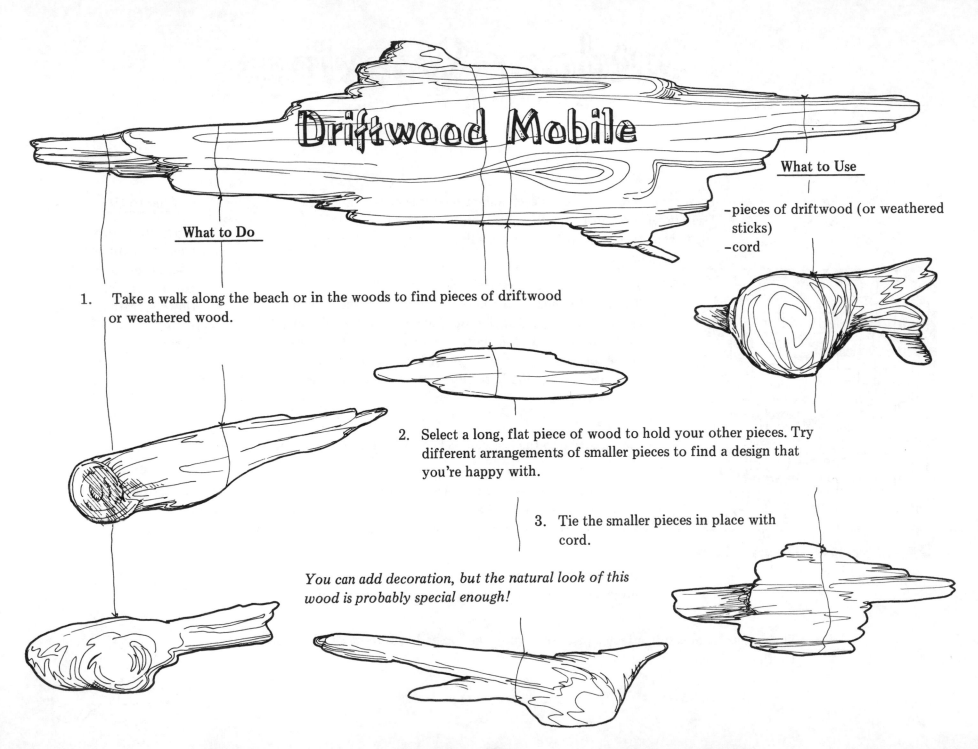

Driftwood Mobile

What to Use

- pieces of driftwood (or weathered sticks)
- cord

What to Do

1. Take a walk along the beach or in the woods to find pieces of driftwood or weathered wood.

2. Select a long, flat piece of wood to hold your other pieces. Try different arrangements of smaller pieces to find a design that you're happy with.

3. Tie the smaller pieces in place with cord.

You can add decoration, but the natural look of this wood is probably special enough!

Bark Necklace

What to Do

1. Search for an interestingly shaped piece of tree bark that is lying on the ground. (You may even be lucky enough to find one with some lichen or insect holes or other unusual features.)

2. Push the darning needle through the bark to make a hole for hanging.

3. Fold the shoelace in half. Thread the two loose ends through the hole from the back of the bark. Leave the folded end free to make a loop. Bring the two loose ends through the loop and pull tightly to hold the bark in place.

4. The shoelace can then be tied in the back to make the necklace the length you want it.

What to Use

- leather shoestring (rayon cord or yarn may be used instead)
- piece of tree bark
- large darning needle

Slingshot

What to Do

What to Use

-sturdy forked branch
-large rubber band or wide sewing elastic
-scrap of sturdy material (canvas or leather)
-pocket knife
-string

1. Find a strong forked branch lying on the ground and trim the forked ends so that they are of equal length. Trim any smaller twigs away with a pocket knife.

2. Cut shallow grooves (wide enough to cradle the rubber band or elastic) one inch from the end of each forked end.

3. Cut the elastic band into two equal lengths and wrap an end of the band around one fork, keeping it flat in the groove you cut. Do the same thing on the other fork with the other piece of band.

4. Secure the tied strips in place with tightly knotted string. Trim excess string to leave ½ inch tails.

5. Cut a rectangle of leather or canvas 4½ by 2 inches. On each short side, cut a slit just a little wider than the width of your elastic.

6. Thread the elastic through the slit and secure with string in the same manner as before, leaving about ½ inch excess. Now you have a super slingshot for tin can target practice! ONLY aim your slingshot at nonliving, nonbreakable targets!

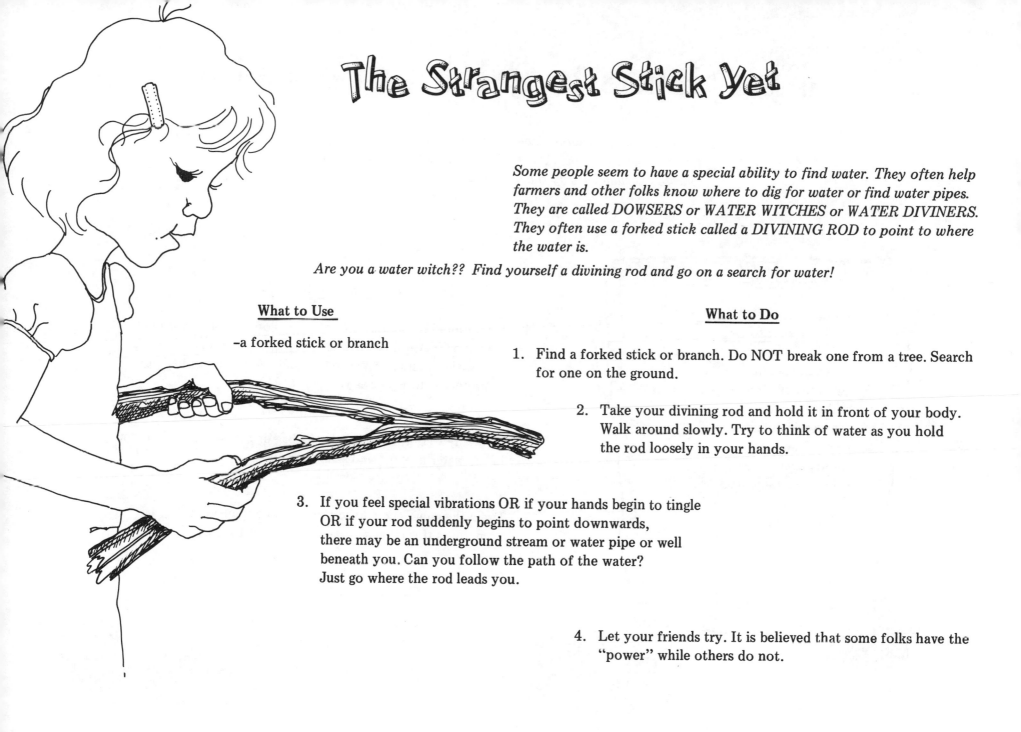

The Strangest Stick Yet

Some people seem to have a special ability to find water. They often help farmers and other folks know where to dig for water or find water pipes. They are called DOWSERS or WATER WITCHES or WATER DIVINERS. They often use a forked stick called a DIVINING ROD to point to where the water is.

Are you a water witch?? Find yourself a divining rod and go on a search for water!

What to Use

–a forked stick or branch

What to Do

1. Find a forked stick or branch. Do NOT break one from a tree. Search for one on the ground.

2. Take your divining rod and hold it in front of your body. Walk around slowly. Try to think of water as you hold the rod loosely in your hands.

3. If you feel special vibrations OR if your hands begin to tingle OR if your rod suddenly begins to point downwards, there may be an underground stream or water pipe or well beneath you. Can you follow the path of the water? Just go where the rod leads you.

4. Let your friends try. It is believed that some folks have the "power" while others do not.

Pine Cones to Brighten Any Fire

As the green and yellow flames shoot up from these specially treated pine cones, they'll surely bring extra warmth to everyone who toasts their toes by the open hearth.

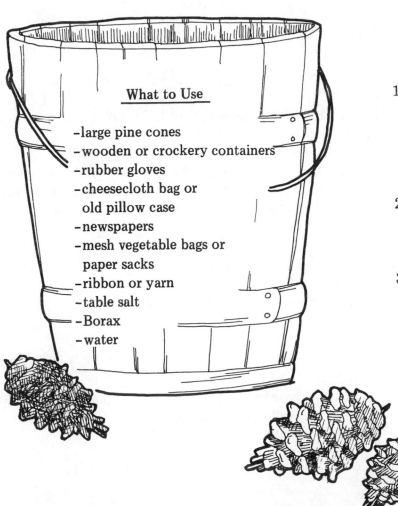

What to Use

- large pine cones
- wooden or crockery containers
- rubber gloves
- cheesecloth bag or old pillow case
- newspapers
- mesh vegetable bags or paper sacks
- ribbon or yarn
- table salt
- Borax
- water

What to Do

1. Put a pound of salt or borax and a gallon of water into the container. <u>Never</u> mix the two chemicals! Salt will give you a yellow flame and borax a green flame. Wear the rubber gloves to protect your hands as you work.

2. Place a few cones at a time in the bag or pillow case. Dip them in the water mixture and soak thoroughly.

3. Drain the cones and spread them on newspapers to dry. Sometimes this takes several days, so don't rush!!

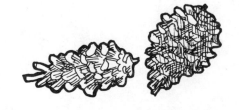

4. When the cones are completely dry, they are ready to be packed in bags for storage. The mesh bags used for oranges and onions are perfect as they allow the air to circulate. If you don't have these, paper bags from the grocery store will do nicely.

5. If the cones are to be used for gifts, the bags should be tied with big, fat ribbon or yarn bows. Add a gift tag cut in a pine cone shape from colored construction paper or old greeting cards.

You can do the same treatment to a small log, and make it into a yule log!

Nuts About Nuts

Carefully open walnut shells. Remove the nut meats and set them aside for later use.

What to Use

- walnut shells
- modeling clay
- scissors
- dimes
- construction paper
- pastel tissue paper or nylon net
- ribbon
- glue
- crayons
- toothpicks

SHIPS TO SAIL ON A PUDDLE SEA!

1. Cut a sail from construction paper.

2. Use crayons to decorate the sail.

3. Glue the sail to a toothpick.

4. Put some modeling clay in the bottom of the walnut shell, and push the end of the toothpick into the clay.

PARTY FAVORS AND DECORATIONS

1. Put a tiny trinket (ring, gum ball, saran-wrapped candy, mini plastic animals, etc.) in a walnut half.

2. Glue the other half of the shell in place.

3. Use for party favors, or tie with ribbon or yarn to hang on a Christmas tree.

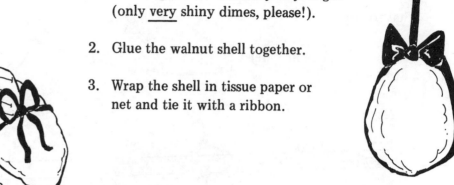

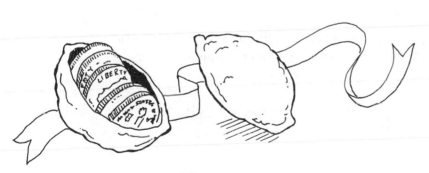

A NOT-TO-BE-FORGOTTEN BIRTHDAY GIFT

1. Put as many dimes in the walnut as the age of the birthday boy or girl (only <u>very</u> shiny dimes, please!).

2. Glue the walnut shell together.

3. Wrap the shell in tissue paper or net and tie it with a ribbon.

OR

Use construction paper, felt-tip pens, and glue to make ears, eyes, tails, noses, fins, mouths, mustaches, wings, legs, etc., to create wondrous walnut wackies!

A Fuzzy Weed Mouse

What to Use

- teasel head or similar weed
- black felt
- glue
- safety pin

What to Do

1. Select a well-shaped teasel head or any other fuzzy weed.

2. Cut two ears, a mouth, two eyes and a tail from black felt.

3. Glue the felt pieces on to form a face. Then glue the tail in place.

4. Glue the safety pin to the back of the weed.

A cocklebur can be used instead of a teasel head. The pin will not be necessary as cockleburs stick to cloth on their own.

Hurrah For Open Spaces!

Outdoor Scavenger Hunt

Plan an outdoor scavenger hunt for your next party, camp–out, or field trip.

What to Do

1. Set the boundaries and time limit for the hunt. Agree on a place to meet when the hunt is over.

2. Choose a timekeeper and judge.

3. Divide the players into partners or teams. Give each group a list that might include:

   - something caught in the wind
   - seed pod
   - tiny pebble
   - something that floats
   - something red
   - feather
   - berry
   - dead leaf
   - piece of wood
   - something yellow
   - something prickly
   - something fuzzy
   - something rough
   - something broken

   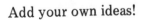

   Add your own ideas!

What to Use

- list of objects to be found (one list for each group)
- clock or watch
- brown paper bag (one for each group)

4. The partners or team back with the most items at the end of the time period are the winners.

Think of a good nature prize!

A Collector's Apron

Wear this apron on your next walk. Put all the things you want to take home with you in the giant pocket so that your hands will be free to keep exploring.

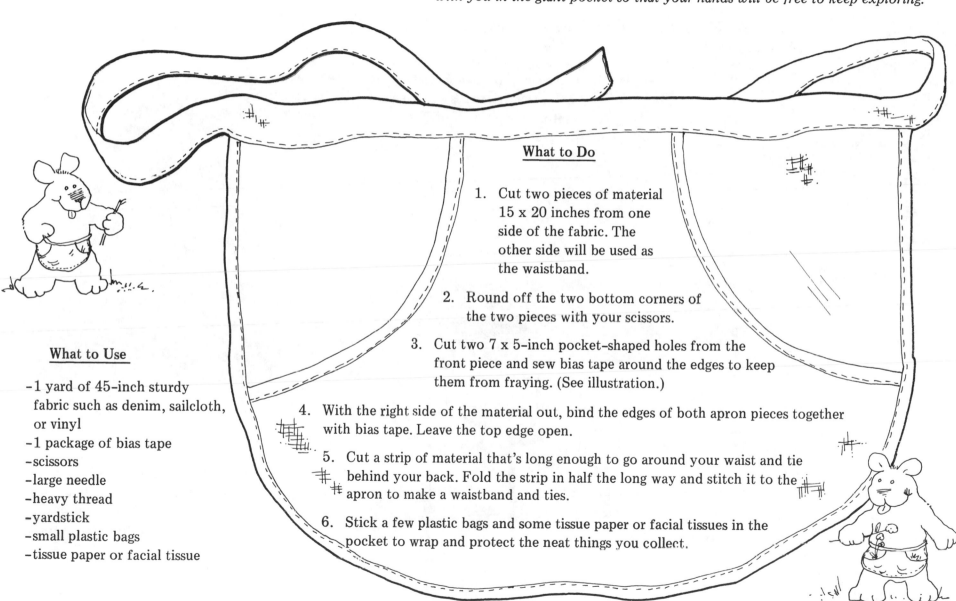

What to Do

1. Cut two pieces of material 15 x 20 inches from one side of the fabric. The other side will be used as the waistband.

2. Round off the two bottom corners of the two pieces with your scissors.

3. Cut two 7 x 5-inch pocket-shaped holes from the front piece and sew bias tape around the edges to keep them from fraying. (See illustration.)

4. With the right side of the material out, bind the edges of both apron pieces together with bias tape. Leave the top edge open.

5. Cut a strip of material that's long enough to go around your waist and tie behind your back. Fold the strip in half the long way and stitch it to the apron to make a waistband and ties.

6. Stick a few plastic bags and some tissue paper or facial tissues in the pocket to wrap and protect the neat things you collect.

What to Use

- 1 yard of 45-inch sturdy fabric such as denim, sailcloth, or vinyl
- 1 package of bias tape
- scissors
- large needle
- heavy thread
- yardstick
- small plastic bags
- tissue paper or facial tissue

Hiding Places...Secret Spaces

Here are some ways that you can create private play places for yourself and your friends.

A tree can provide a special, private place for you alone. Look for a tree that's easy to climb and has a secure, comfortable place to sit. A tree-space is a wonderful place for reading or daydreaming.

FORT ONE
123

Build a fort from cardboard boxes of many sizes. Cut holes for windows or doors or secret entry ways.

Build a clubhouse beneath a ladder! Tape long strips of paper to the top of a ladder. Then fasten the bottoms of the strips to the ground with sticks or rocks.

Find an open space in the center of some bushes or trees.
Use this hideaway as a place to think or sleep or write or play.

Drape old sheets and blankets over a picnic table or card table to make a tent.

Make your own teepee! Tie four poles together at the top with sturdy string (broom handles work well). Stick the ends into the ground. Then cover the frame with newspapers taped together. Paint the outside, if you wish. And don't forget to leave a flap that opens for a door!

Leafy Lodges

When fall winds begin to blow and those autumn leaves come tumbling down, sweep up some leafy piles to use as special play places.

What to Use

- broom or rake
- fallen leaves
- lots of imagination

What to Do

1. Sweep up lots of leaves and shape them into the outline of a house. Make walls for the rooms. Remember to leave open spaces in your walls for doorways.

2. Make a castle, a dungeon, a spaceship, or anything else you want. You can change the shape of your outline to make anything.

3. Try making leaf furniture. Cover a pile of leaves with an old sheet to make a giant bed or chair.

4. When you have finished playing in your leaf house, scatter the leaves back over the ground for protection or rake them into a pile for burning, bagging, or composting.

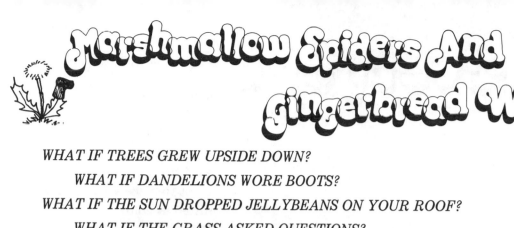

Marshmallow Spiders And Gingerbread Wind

WHAT IF TREES GREW UPSIDE DOWN?

WHAT IF DANDELIONS WORE BOOTS?

WHAT IF THE SUN DROPPED JELLYBEANS ON YOUR ROOF?

WHAT IF THE GRASS ASKED QUESTIONS?

WHAT IF CLOUDS WERE VEGETABLE SOUP?

WHAT IF THE WIND TASTED LIKE GINGERBREAD?

WHAT IF FOUNTAINS SQUIRTED FROM EVERY SIDEWALK?

WHAT IF ICICLES GREW IN YOUR GARDEN?

WHAT IF LIGHTNING CAME AND RESTED IN YOUR WAGON?

WHAT IF YOU COULD CARRY STARS IN YOUR LUNCHBOX?

WHAT IF ALL INSECTS PLAYED MUSICAL INSTRUMENTS?

WHAT IF SPIDERS WERE MADE OF MARSHMALLOW?

WHAT IF YOU WERE AS SMALL AS A MOSQUITO?

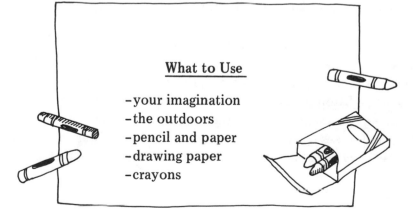

What to Use

- your imagination
- the outdoors
- pencil and paper
- drawing paper
- crayons

What to Do

1. Look out your window or walk through your yard or watch around you as you hike. As you look, imagine that things are different. Ask yourself: "What if . . . . ?" about everything you see.

2. Create your own list of outdoor "What Ifs?" Close your eyes and use your imagination to decide what it would be like if the "What Ifs?" were true! Draw what you see!

a Marathon for Everyone

Lots of folks can be involved in this kind of a marathon.
Find out who wants to participate—and start planning the events!

What to Use

- lots of people
- equipment needed for the events planned
- a wooden stick or baton for each team
- paint to make each baton a different color
- starting line
- finishing line

What to Do

1. Start by getting a list of all the people who want to join in. Divide the people into two or more teams. Try to balance the teams so that each includes members of different ages.

2. Decide what the events will be and assign an event to each team member. Match the people to events according to their ability to do the event. These pages will give you ideas for some of the events you might include. You can add other activities, too.

3. Decide the order of events and set up the course so that all the necessary equipment can be ready at the spot where each event will occur.

4. Choose a time and day for the marathon. Give everyone a chance to practice his or her event ahead of time.

5. Here's the way the marathon will work. All members of both teams take their places along the marathon route. Those doing the first event begin at the starting line at the same time, each holding a baton in one hand. When a member has finished her event she passes the baton to the next team member. He does his task and passes it on. The baton may be laid down during the event if necessary. This continues until all the events are completed.

6. Have a great marathon!!

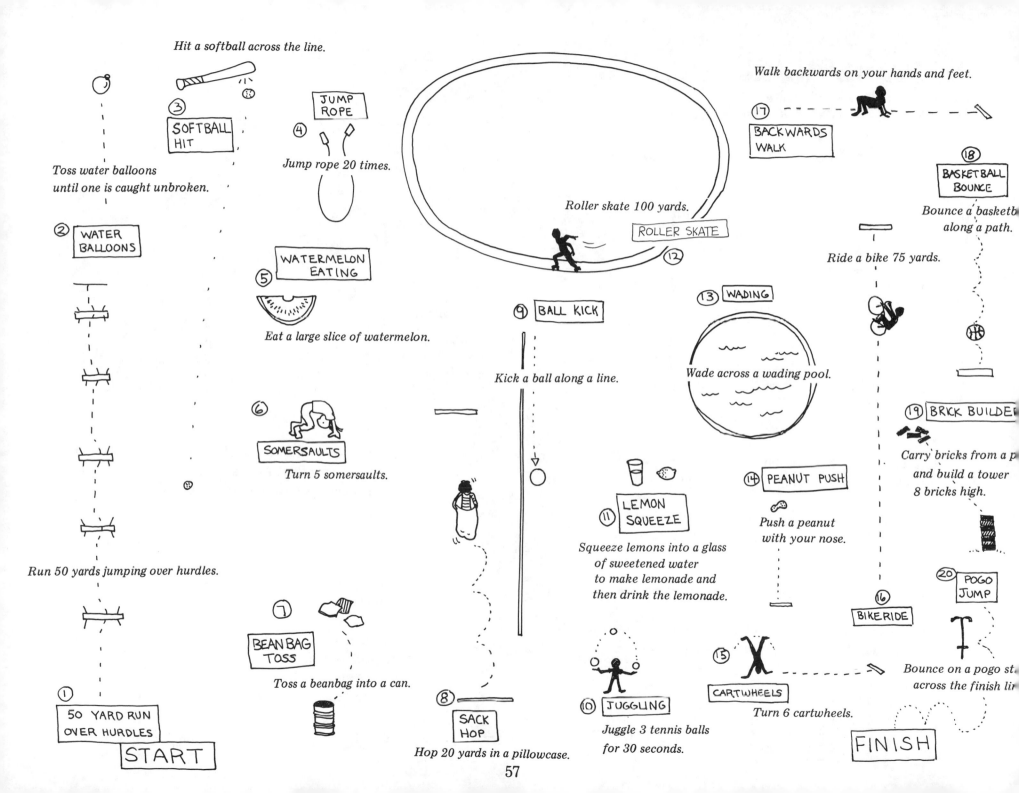

Hit a softball across the line.

③ SOFTBALL HIT

JUMP ROPE
④
Jump rope 20 times.

Toss water balloons until one is caught unbroken.

② WATER BALLOONS

⑤ WATERMELON EATING

Eat a large slice of watermelon.

⑥

SOMERSAULTS

Turn 5 somersaults.

Run 50 yards jumping over hurdles.

⑦

BEAN BAG TOSS

Toss a beanbag into a can.

①

50 YARD RUN OVER HURDLES

START

⑧

SACK HOP

Hop 20 yards in a pillowcase.

⑨ BALL KICK

Kick a ball along a line.

⑪ LEMON SQUEEZE

Squeeze lemons into a glass of sweetened water to make lemonade and then drink the lemonade.

⑩ JUGGLING

Juggle 3 tennis balls for 30 seconds.

Roller skate 100 yards.

ROLLER SKATE

⑫

⑬ WADING

Wade across a wading pool.

⑭ PEANUT PUSH

Push a peanut with your nose.

⑮ CARTWHEELS

Turn 6 cartwheels.

Walk backwards on your hands and feet.

⑰ BACKWARDS WALK

⑱ BASKETBALL BOUNCE

Bounce a basketb along a path.

Ride a bike 75 yards.

⑲ BRICK BUILDE

Carry bricks from a p and build a tower 8 bricks high.

⑳ POGO JUMP

Bounce on a pogo st across the finish li

⑯ BIKE RIDE

FINISH

57

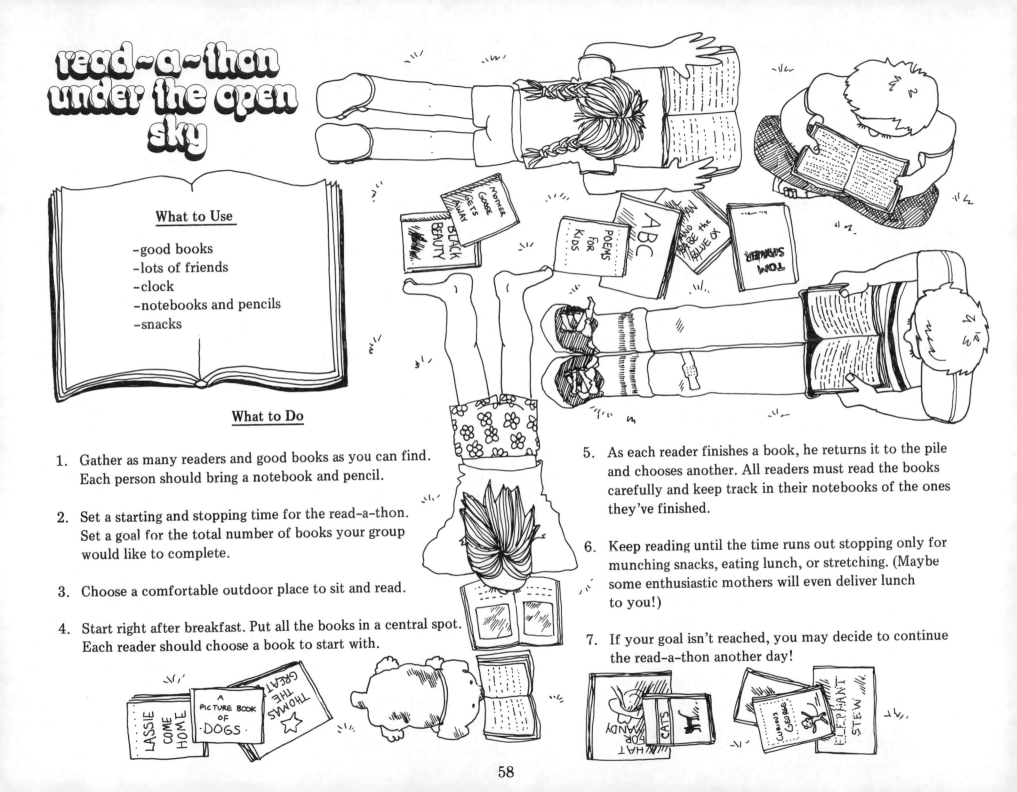

read-a-thon under the open sky

What to Use

- good books
- lots of friends
- clock
- notebooks and pencils
- snacks

What to Do

1. Gather as many readers and good books as you can find. Each person should bring a notebook and pencil.

2. Set a starting and stopping time for the read-a-thon. Set a goal for the total number of books your group would like to complete.

3. Choose a comfortable outdoor place to sit and read.

4. Start right after breakfast. Put all the books in a central spot. Each reader should choose a book to start with.

5. As each reader finishes a book, he returns it to the pile and chooses another. All readers must read the books carefully and keep track in their notebooks of the ones they've finished.

6. Keep reading until the time runs out stopping only for munching snacks, eating lunch, or stretching. (Maybe some enthusiastic mothers will even deliver lunch to you!)

7. If your goal isn't reached, you may decide to continue the read-a-thon another day!

Good Books Belong Outdoors!

Here are a few suggestions for taking some of our favorite books outdoors!

* Find a stretch of sidewalk to sit on and share *WHERE THE SIDEWALK ENDS by Shel Silverstein* with a friend who likes to giggle.

* Curl up under the shade of a leafy tree to enjoy *CHARLOTTE'S WEB by E. B. White.*

* Tuck a copy of *IF I WERE IN CHARGE OF THE WORLD* (poems for children and their parents) *by Judith Viorst* in the family picnic basket.

* Bag a lunch, wear quiet shoes, grab your binoculars, hang on to *BIRDS (from the Golden Guide to Nature Series),* and head out for an afternoon of bird watching.

* Spend an afternoon making kites, painting with water, catching shadows or trying any number of other wonderful outdoor projects with the no-fail directions you'll find in *I CAN MAKE A RAINBOW by Marjorie Frank.*

* Save *THE SIERRA CLUB SUMMER BOOK by Linda Allison* for the hottest two weeks of the summer.

* Take a flashlight, a very special grown-up friend and *THE NIGHT SKY BOOK by Jamie Jobb* outside on the next clear night.

* On your next hike, pack some of the four tiny *NUTSHELL LIBRARY* books *by Maurice Sendak* in your knapsack or backpack. You'll be able to enjoy them at rest time.

* Stretch out on your stomach beside a stream or pond one lazy spring day with *THE ADVENTURES OF HUCKLEBERRY FINN* or *THE ADVENTURES OF TOM SAWYER by Mark Twain.*

* *ON CITY STREETS by Nancy Larrick* (poems about the sights and sounds and people of the city) is just right for reading or memorizing as you pause to people-watch on a busy sidewalk.

* Do yoga under the open sky with help from *Rachel Carr's BE A FROG, A BIRD, OR A TREE.*

* Read *IN GRANNY'S GARDEN by Sarah Harrison and Mike Wilks* before you begin the search for your own enchanted garden.

* The *GUINNESS BOOK OF WORLD RECORDS* makes exciting treehouse reading. Then you'll want to get down from the tree and set some of your own records.

* When you've had the very worst day of your life, take *ALEXANDER AND THE TERRIBLE, HORRIBLE, NO GOOD VERY BAD DAY by Judith Viorst* and go for a walk all by yourself!

Do You Hear What I Hear?

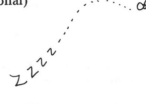

What to Use

- notebook and pencil
- tape recorder (optional)

CHEE ·· CHEE ··

BUZZZ

ZZZZ

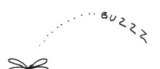

What to Do

1. Find a place where you can sit very still. Sit with your eyes closed so you can listen without being distracted by the sights around you.

2. Concentrate on the sounds you hear. Try to collect sounds in your notebook, in your head, or on your tape recorder.

   Can you hear   *rustling?*   *whimpering?*   *singing?*
                   whistling?   *sighing?*   *thumping?*
                   swishing?   *hissing?*   *buzzing?*
                   screeching? *scampering?*   *groaning?*

3. Decide which sounds are natural sounds and which ones are manmade sounds.

4. Listen for outside sounds and sounds coming from inside.

5. Concentrate on the soft, subtle sounds as well as the loud ones.

6. Listen for sounds above you, around you, beneath you. Try putting your ear to the ground against a tree, near a fire hydrant, beside a stream.

How many sounds can you collect?
Can you identify the sounds?

On a Clear Day

What to Use

- acrylic paints
- paint brushes
- water and rags
- piece of clear glass or plastic
- masking tape
- clear day
- two bricks

What to Do

1. Tape around the edges of the glass or plastic so that you won't hurt yourself on any rough edges.

2. Carry the glass outside and look through it. Move around until you see an interesting sight that you would like to paint.

3. Set the glass down on a box, flat rock, or table. Place it in a position that will allow you to see your scene through the glass. Put a brick on either side of the glass to hold it up.

4. Paint right on the glass exactly what you see through it. This will be almost like tracing what's on the other side.

5. Let the painting dry, then hang it in a window!

61

Obstacle Course

What to Use

- clock or stopwatch
- old boxes, ropes, ladders, balls, and other equipment needed for obstacles you design
- friends

What to Do

1. Find or make several things to use as obstacles.

2. Decide what activities can be done with each obstacle. You can use some of the ideas on these pages and add some of your own.

3. Find an open space and set up your obstacle course. Practice running it a few times.

4. Have a friend time you as you do the course. Keep track of your time. Try to improve it next time.

5. Try rearranging the obstacle course to make it more difficult. This will provide a new challenge once you've mastered the first course.

Brush up on body skills and have a lot of fun at the same time with your own homemade obstacle course.

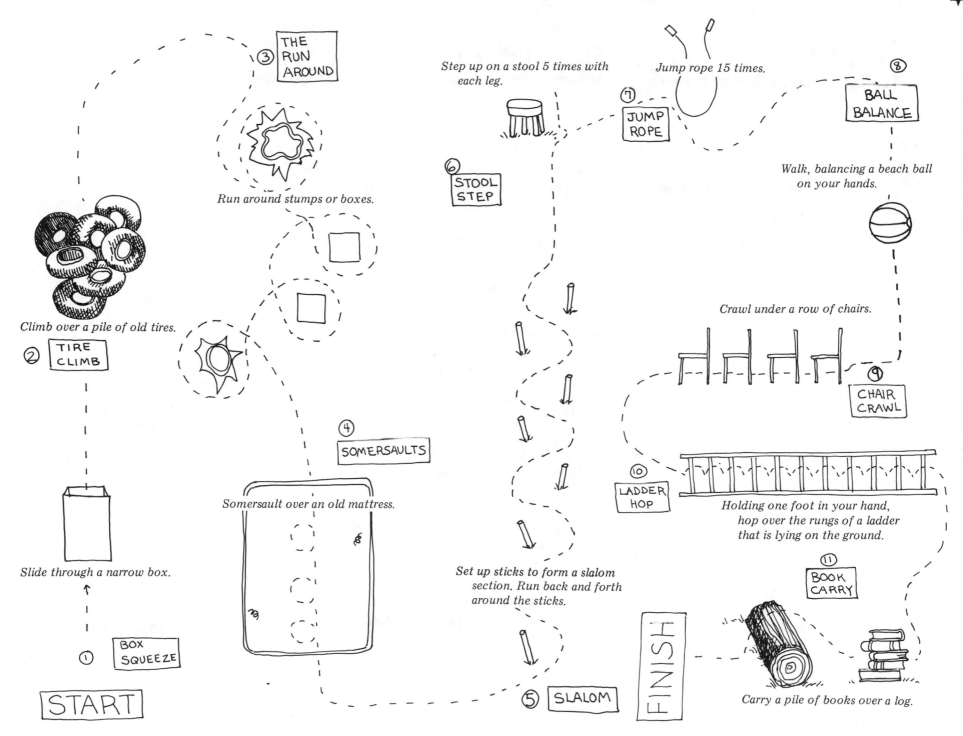

③ **THE RUN AROUND**

Step up on a stool 5 times with each leg.

Jump rope 15 times.

⑧ **BALL BALANCE**

Run around stumps or boxes.

⑥ **STOOL STEP**

⑦ **JUMP ROPE**

Walk, balancing a beach ball on your hands.

Climb over a pile of old tires.

② **TIRE CLIMB**

Crawl under a row of chairs.

⑨ **CHAIR CRAWL**

④ **SOMERSAULTS**

Somersault over an old mattress.

⑩ **LADDER HOP**

Holding one foot in your hand, hop over the rungs of a ladder that is lying on the ground.

Slide through a narrow box.

Set up sticks to form a slalom section. Run back and forth around the sticks.

⑪ **BOOK CARRY**

① **BOX SQUEEZE**

START

⑤ **SLALOM**

FINISH

Carry a pile of books over a log.

Collecting is Contagious

KIDS ARE COLLECTORS!! We know a girl who collects police badges and a boy who collects elephants (not live ones!). What do you collect? The out-of-doors gives kids lots of space and time for the snooping and visiting and trading that helps build collections. Start a collection today—or add to one you've already started!

WALL DRUG

MINNESOTA 1967
SPV-184
LAND OF 10,000 LAKES

What to Use

- ideas on the next page
- containers for collecting and displaying items you gather

What to Do

1. Decide what you want to collect. You can collect ALMOST ANYTHING!! See some of the ideas on the next page to help you get started.

2. Go looking in attics, drawers, cellars, trash cans. Visit garage sales, swap meets, flea markets, and rummage sales. Talk to your friends about collecting. They are a great source of good stuff. You can trade collectibles with each other.

3. Find a way to organize the treasures you've collected. You can store them in boxes, envelopes, or scrapbooks. Or you might display them on posters, shelves, or in display cases.

SOME THINGS TO COLLECT

buttons	T-shirts
masks	models
marbles	nails
hats	pillows
kites	keys
coupons	menus
postcards	greeting cards
gum wrappers	sports cards
bumper stickers	stamps
posters	coins
labels	cans
stickers	matchbook covers
autographs	flags
rocks	records
corks	badges
fingerprints	shells
patches	puppets
dolls	rubber stamps
footprints	comic books
bottles	photographs
teacups	license plates
	spoons

More ideas of your own:

_____ _____

_____ _____

_____ _____

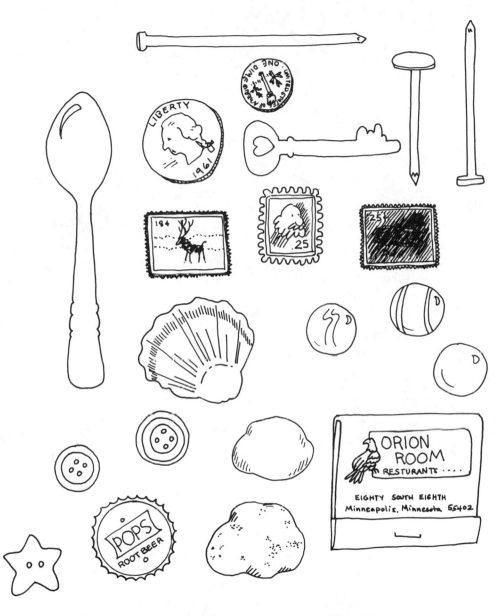

Visit your library and look at the ENCYCLOPEDIA OF ASSOCIATIONS. It will give you information about groups of people who share different hobbies. Join a hobby group to find out more about your own kind of collecting!

Mapmakers on the Loose

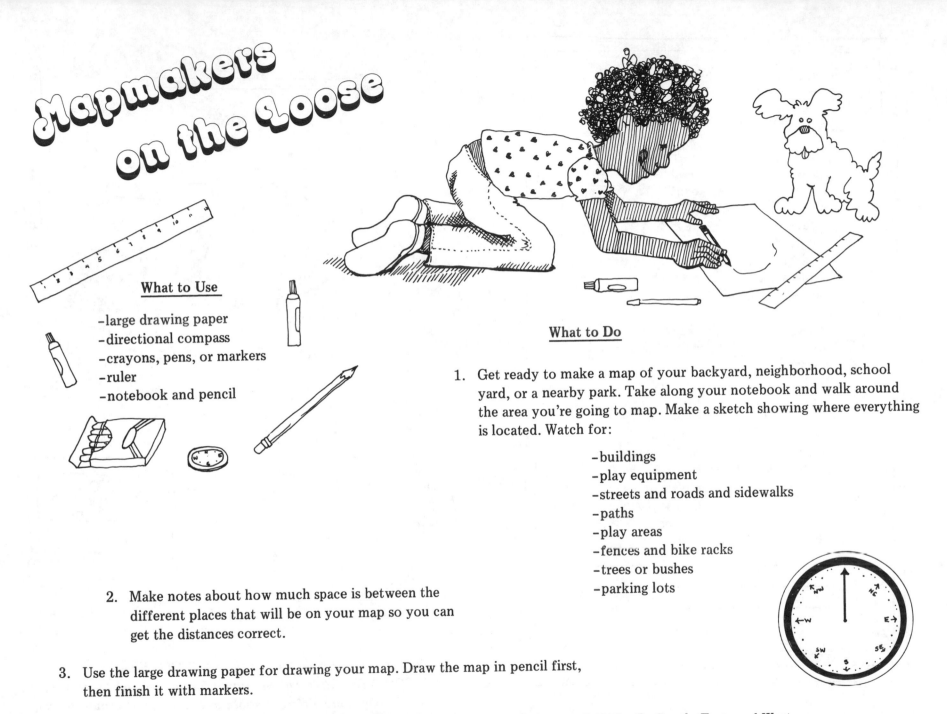

What to Use

- large drawing paper
- directional compass
- crayons, pens, or markers
- ruler
- notebook and pencil

What to Do

1. Get ready to make a map of your backyard, neighborhood, school yard, or a nearby park. Take along your notebook and walk around the area you're going to map. Make a sketch showing where everything is located. Watch for:

   - buildings
   - play equipment
   - streets and roads and sidewalks
   - paths
   - play areas
   - fences and bike racks
   - trees or bushes
   - parking lots

2. Make notes about how much space is between the different places that will be on your map so you can get the distances correct.

3. Use the large drawing paper for drawing your map. Draw the map in pencil first, then finish it with markers.

4. Make sure you give your map a title, a key, and directions. Use a compass to help you find North, South, East, and West.

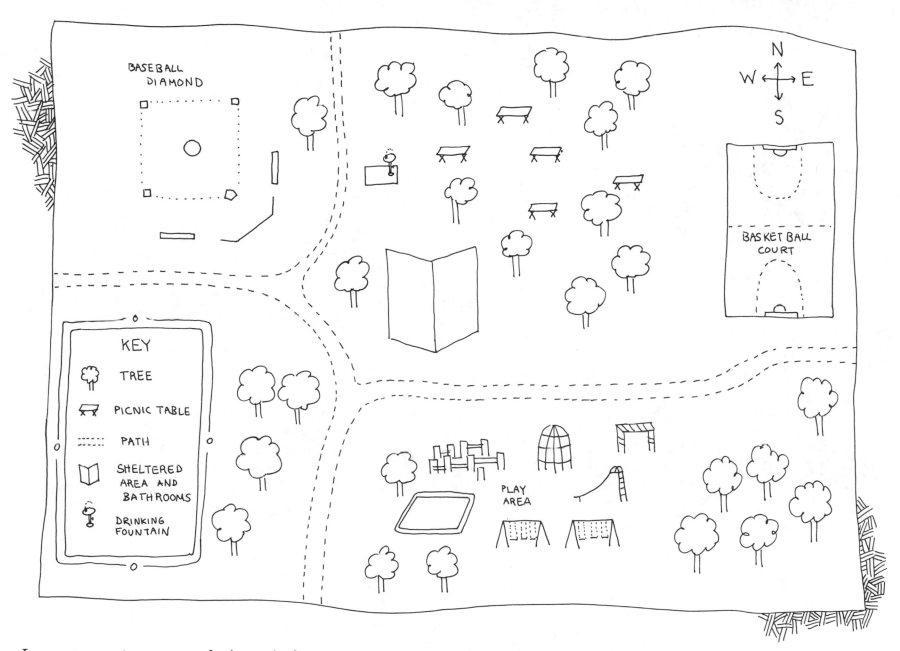

Loan your map to someone who is new in the area.
See if your map can help her to find her way around!

Hey, how about trying a 3-dimensional map!!

Oversized, Overstuffed Blocks

What to Do

1. Crumple up a lot of old newspapers. Fill several grocery bags almost to the top with the crumpled papers.

2. Fold over the top of each bag and tape or staple it closed securely.

3. Use your BIG BLOCKS for tossing in the air, building towers, playing games, or making obstacle courses.

4. TRY THIS: Have several people lie on their backs, each kicking a BIG BLOCK up in the air. See who can hold the block up the longest without letting it touch the ground.

What to Use

- lots of newspapers
- large grocery bags
- wide masking tape or stapler
- scissors

USE YOUR NOSE!

What to Use

-small paper bag
-clover, moss, bark, wild ginger roots,
  mint leaves, onion tops, grass, flowers, etc.
  (Only use things you KNOW are safe to taste.
  Ask an adult if you're not sure about something.)
-blindfolds

What to Do

1. Gather together a few people to play this game. Divide into groups of two.

2. Put each item into a separate bag.

3. Blindfold one person in each group.

4. Have the other person in the group hold the bag up to his partner's nose. The blindfolded person tries to guess what's in the bag by the way it smells. If he can't guess by smell, then he tastes the object and guesses again. If he still doesn't know what it is, then he feels the object. As soon as he guesses what's in the bag, the other person takes a turn at smelling, tasting, and touching.

Batting Brush-Up

What to Use

- soft ball (such as a tennis ball or wiffle ball)
- bat (preferably plastic)
- thin rope
- heavy string
- scissors

What to Do

1. Hang a rope between two trees that are at least eight feet apart. Keep the rope tight and hang it about the same height as the top of your head.

2. Tie a string around the ball and hang it from the rope so that the ball is about level with your waist.

3. Get your bat and start hitting the ball. Each time you hit it, the ball will return right to you ready for the next hit!

This way you can practice batting any time of year, even indoors!

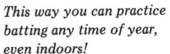

Imitation Fossils

Fossils are imprints of animals, fish, or plants that lived thousands of years ago. The animal or plant was caught in hot volcanic lava that quickly cooled into rock. Because fossils are old, they tell us how life on the earth used to be.

See if you can find some fossils on your next walk. In the meantime, make a pretend fossil of your own.

What to Do

1. Cut two ovals out of the cardboard. Cut a hole out of one of the ovals to make a frame.

2. Cover both sides of the leaf or fern frond with Vaseline and place it on the cardboard oval.

3. Place the frame on top and tape the two pieces of cardboard together.

4. Pour the plaster of Paris over the leaf and cover the entire surface exposed in the oval cut-out.

5. When the plaster of Paris hardens, remove both cardboard pieces to free your fossil.

What to Use

- leaf or fern frond
- heavy corrugated cardboard
- scissors
- masking tape
- Vaseline
- plaster of Paris

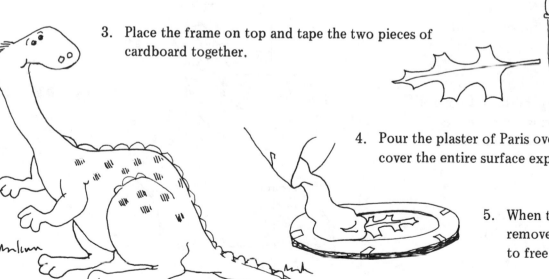

Measure Wherever You Go

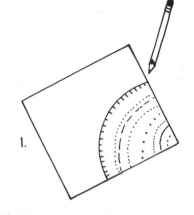

1.

What to Do

1. Trace the shape on the next page four times onto tracing paper.
   Trace it exactly as it is drawn. Use a fine-point marker to put all the
   markings on the shape exactly as they are shown.

2. Cut out your tracings carefully. Glue them onto the cardboard so
   that they form a circle. Then cut carefully around the outside
   of the circle.

3. Draw an arrow from the center of the circle straight down to one
   edge. Start numbering (with a marker) by marking 1 cm. on the
   first dot to the left of the arrow. Continue numbering all the way
   around. You should get to 100 cm. when you get back around
   to the arrow.

4. Nail your measuring wheel to the stick by pounding the nail
   loosely through the center of the wheel and into the stick.
   You want the wheel to turn easily.

What to Use

- large piece of heavy cardboard
- sturdy scissors
- 4 pieces of tracing paper or typing paper
- centimeter ruler
- permanent markers
- pencil
- glue
- yardstick or dowel about the same size
- large nail and hammer

2.
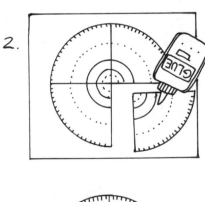

3.
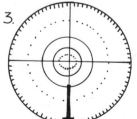

4.
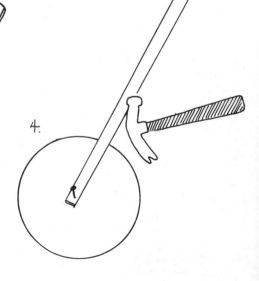

5. Now you're ready to measure. Start with the arrow pointing down. Walk along and count the number of times the arrow goes completely around. Each turn equals 100 centimeters or 1 meter. Any extra distance will show in centimeters.

HOW FAR DO YOU TRAVEL . . . .

to school?
around your yard?
around your house?
to your friend's house?
to the bus stop?
to the park?
around the block?

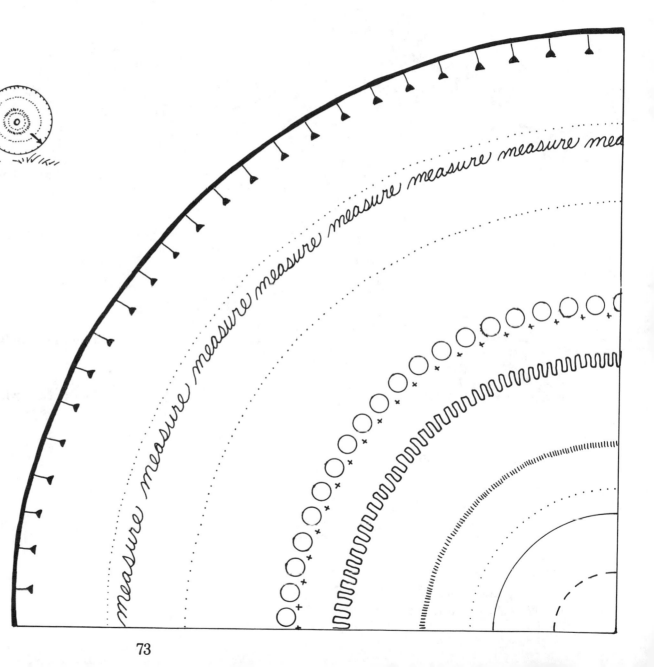

73

Hold Your Ears!

SAMSON

What to Use

-thin paper
-scissors
-crayons or markers (optional)

What to Do

1. Cut a long, thin strip of paper. Fold the strip in half.

2. Cut a small hole in the folded edge of the strip.

3. Fold the bottom edges of the strip up. (See example.)

4. Color or decorate your whistle, if you'd like to.

5. GO OUTSIDE. Hold the ends of the whistle loosely between two fingers. Blow hard into the folded paper. The air will make the paper vibrate and cause a screeching whistle!

Always use this whistle outside. Never blow it close to someone's ears.

Try these changes to see what sounds you get:

longer or shorter paper
bigger or smaller hole
thicker paper
wider or skinnier strip

Try a Tug-of-War

ANYONE CAN PLAY TUG-OF-WAR! *Get the whole family or the neighborhood out for this good old-fashioned fun.*

What to Do

1. Draw a winning line or place a marker down the center of the tugging area.

2. Divide the people into two teams. All the folks on a team should line up on one end of the rope starting about 10 feet from the center.

3. At the GO signal, both teams start pulling.

4. A team wins when the first member of the other team is pulled across the winning line.

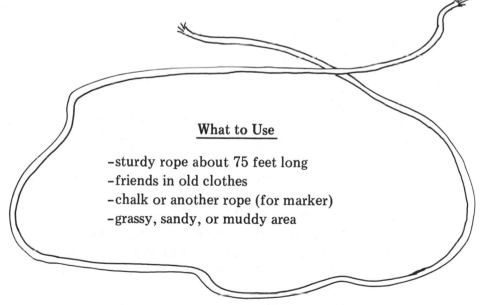

What to Use

-sturdy rope about 75 feet long
-friends in old clothes
-chalk or another rope (for marker)
-grassy, sandy, or muddy area

For extra fun, try a tug-of-war across a stream or through a sprinkler!

Do the Grapevine Swing!

In many places wild grapevines grow so thick and hang so low from trees that you can grab hold of one and have a grand time swinging! Look for a grapevine swing in your area, or make your own outdoor swing!

What to Do

1. When you find a grapevine, test it with several hard tugs to see that it is strong enough to support your weight. Check to see that it is securely fastened above on a tree.

2. Once you're sure it's safe . . . you can start swinging!

OR

1. If you can't find a grapevine for swinging, you can make your own swing from a heavy rope. Choose a long rope that is very sturdy.

2. Have an adult help you fasten the rope to a strong tree branch.

3. Tie a huge knot in the end of the rope that hangs near the ground. You can sit or stand on the knot when you swing. OR you can put the rope through a center hole in a round piece of wood. Tie a large knot underneath the wood, and you'll have a nice seat for your swing!

What to Use

-sturdy, hanging grapevine
 OR
-heavy rope 8–10 feet long
-12-inch diameter piece of sturdy wood with hole cut in middle (optional)
-adult help

Ode to the Great Outdoors

Write a poem celebrating the great outdoors!

What to Do

1. Start thinking about all the wonderful things and experiences offered to you by the outdoors. Make a list of sounds, sights, feelings, smells, tastes, adventures, and lessons that the outdoors supplies. Your list can have words or phrases or ideas. Write your list on a large piece of posterboard.

2. Lean your idea list against a tree or set it in a spot where you can see the list. Look over the list and choose the most interesting or unusual or favorite items on the list. Include these in your poem.

3. Begin writing by following this form (or make up a form of your own.)

What to Use

- paper and pencil
- posterboard
- marker

HURRAH FOR THE GREAT OUTDOORS!!

For _____

And _____

For _____

And _____

I love the _____

And the _____

HURRAH FOR THE GREAT OUTDOORS!!

An Old-Fashioned Block Party

Make plans for a party that includes EVERYONE on your block or street. It's a great way to get to know the folks in your neighborhood while everyone has a good time.

What to Use

- invitations
- equipment needed for games and activities
- good food
- decorations
- lots of neighbors

GAMES · CONTESTS · FUN · GOOD FOOD · GREAT PEOPLE

COME TO THE MAPLE ST. SUMMER BASH

SATURDAY, JUNE 27, 7:00 P.M.

Right in the middle of Maple Street

BRING: sports equipment, food for pot luck, your own drinks.

WEAR: Old comfortable clothes

R.S.V.P.
John + Joni
661·3111

If it rains come next Sat.

What to Do

1. Choose a time for your BLOCK PARTY. Often a Saturday or Sunday afternoon is a good time. Ask an adult for advice on this.

2. Decide where to hold it. You can do it outside on the sidewalks or in an empty lot or in someone's backyard. In some towns you can close off the street so your party can take place right in the street. Call your local police station for permission.

3. Plan the games and events. Try to plan activities that can include all ages and abilities and interests. (See the next page for ideas.)

4. Decide on a menu. Ask people to share in providing the food.

5. Make invitations to send to all the families on the block.
   Be sure to tell: The day and time
   The place
   What to bring
   What to wear
   What to expect

6. Gather all the equipment and decorations you'll need and get set up for the party. Then have a wonderful time! !

EVENTS

- Whistling Contest 1:00
- Watermelon Eating Race
- Jumproping
- New Games
- Baby Race
- Double Decker Wrestling
- Tug of War

- Pie Throwing Contest
- Balloon Tail Tag
- Beachball Volleyball
- Touch Football
- Kick the Can
- Egg Toss
- Street Soccer

Pack Up for a Picnic

A picnic is fun anytime. You can go to a park or a forest preserve, or enjoy a picnic right on your own back step. The next time you're packing up for a picnic, try one of these picnic menus.

What to Use

- picnic food
- containers and wrappers for food
- picnic basket, bag, or backpack
- cups, forks, knives, spoons
- plates, napkins

PUT-TOGETHER-LATER SALAD

Take along any of the following:

lettuce	fresh spinach
endive	other salad
pepper slices	greens
carrot chunks	cucumber slices
sprouts	celery hunks
cheese cubes	zucchini strips
tomato slices	sunflower seeds
	olives

When you're ready to eat, toss everything together. Add a squeeze of lemon juice and enjoy! Finish off the meal with a drink and an oatmeal cookie.

BREADS & SPREADS

Take bread or crackers or rolls. Spread on any of these:

applesauce	honey
peanut butter	butter
egg salad	cottage cheese
cream cheese	yogurt
tuna salad	apple butter
squashed bananas	sour cream

Top with any of these:

sprouts	olives
cucumber slices	wheat germ
poppy seeds	sunflower seeds
pickles	granola
raisins	currants
nuts	sesame seeds
chopped green pepper	shredded carrots

**Don't forget a dessert and drink!

STOP & DIP

Take a container of yogurt and dillweed or cottage cheese mixed with crushed pineapple.

Dip any of these into your creamy dip:

green onions	carrot sticks
olives	zucchini fingers
apple rings	chips
pickles	celery chunks
cucumber slices	banana slices
orange sections	cheese slices
bread sticks	hunks of bread
crackers	fingers

Take along a drink and dessert, too!

Picnics Are Not Just For Summer

Don't overlook a picnic just because the weather is cool. On a crisp, fall day, hike to a forest and rest on a log. OR, make a shelter from the wind on a snowy day and sit down on a thick blanket to spread out your picnic. OR, take a lunch outside for a sidewalk snack on a cool spring day.

COOL WEATHER PICNIC MENU

* thermos jugs full of hot soup or stew or chile

* hot, spiced tea or hot chocolate in thermos jugs

* muffins, buttered and wrapped in foil

* chunks of cheese on toothpicks

* whole carrots, cleaned

* big fat cookies or brownies or graham crackers

What to Do

1. Pack up your food. Make sure drinks and soups are hot. Wrap everything well and put it in a basket or bag for carrying.

2. Take along a large piece of plastic to use as your table and seat. This will serve as a cover for any damp or cold ground.

3. Dress warmly since you'll be sitting still while you eat.

4. Use straws for your drinks. Everything on this menu can be eaten without even taking off your mittens!

What to Use

- food from picnic menu
- straws
- spoons
- large plastic garbage bag or other piece of plastic
- warm clothes

Outdoor Theater

When the weather is warm, the time is just right for outdoor performances. Here are some things to do to get ready for putting on shows of your own.

What to Do

1. Round up your actors. You may include kids, grown-ups, puppets, robots, and even animals.

2. Decide what kind of a performance you'll do. You might consider:

   > puppet shows
   > plays
   > original dramas
   > talent shows

What to Use

- friends
- materials for stage, scenery, costumes
- paper, pens, cardboard to make posters and tickets
- chairs

3. Find a stage. You can use a garage as the stage with the garage door serving as a curtain. Or make a theater from large pieces of cardboard. One easy way to create a backyard stage is by hanging sheets from a clothesline.

4. Create your scenery. You can use paper and paint and cardboard and fabric to make all sorts of props for the performance. Borrow furniture and other items from inside your house only with permission.

SALTINE CRACKERS

5. Make costumes. You can design almost any kind of costume
   by using:

   -paper bags
   -large plastic garbage bags
   -large cardboard boxes
   -old sheets
   -old pillowcases
   -paper
   -old clothes
   -fabric, yarn
   -aluminum foil

6. Rehearse your performance. Practice until you feel ready to perform in public.

7. Set a time for the theater to open. Advertise the performance and sell or give away tickets. Set up chairs or a space for the audience to sit.

8. Have a grand time!

Hit the Trail

Good stuff to know . . . . for campers and hikers!

GETTING READY

1. Plan your trip well. Get maps ahead of time and decide where you'll go, where you'll camp and how long it will take.

2. Break in your hiking boots or shoes ahead of time. New boots can be dreadful to the feet on a hike! Wear them around the house or yard several times before going on a long hike.

3. Check all your camping equipment to make sure nothing is damaged or missing.

4. Make a checklist of things you'll need to take. Remember that everything you take has to be carried on your back! Take what you need to be safe and comfortable but don't take too much.

5. Start packing. Make sure you leave these things near the top so you can easily reach them:

    rainwear   first aid kit   toilet paper

         snack   water

6. Let someone know where you're going, and take a friend along. It isn't a good idea to hike alone.

√ warm clothes
√ cool clothes
√ extra socks
√ rain gear
√ boots
√ compass
√ bug repellant
   sun screen
√ flashlight
   matches
√ whistle
√ snack for trail
√ food for camp

√ toilet paper
   first aid kit
√ pocket knife
   rope
   water
√ sleeping bag
   cooking pots
   personal items
   tent (optional)
   camera (optional)

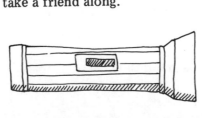

ON THE TRAIL

1. Stay on the trail while you're hiking. Watch the trail markers so that you don't lose the trail.

2. If you begin to feel burning anywhere on your feet, STOP IMMEDIATELY and put moleskin on those "hot spots." Don't let those blisters get started!

3. Eat and drink a little along the way. It's important to keep water in your body and keep up your energy with nutritious food.

4. Don't run or push too hard. Rest when you need to. Take at least one long rest, perhaps for lunch. Take the time to enjoy yourself and the scenery!

5. Leave the surroundings undisturbed. Don't pick any plants or carry away animals from their habitat.

6. Never eat any berries or mushrooms or plants along the way. Even if you think they're edible, it's safer not to take the chance.

7. Remember not to litter. Carry all your trash home with you.

8. If you get warm hiking, take off one layer of clothes. If you get cold, add a layer. Don't allow yourself to be so warm that you sweat up your clothes because when you stop hiking, the wet clothes may give you a chill.

IN CAMP

1. Set up your tent first. Choose a spot that's flat and free from rocks. Camp away from water in a place that isn't likely to collect water if it rains.

2. Never take food in your tent or leave it lying around the camp if you've seen animals around. Pack it up tightly and hang it high on a branch.

3. Keep the tent closed when you're away from camp. That way you won't collect any unwelcome visitors or rain in your tent!

4. When you use toilet paper, bury it or burn it.

5. Enjoy your stay! Relax, read, tell stories, and starwatch.

6. Leave for home in plenty of time.

7. Leave your campsite clean. Try to make it look as though you were never there!

IF YOU GET LOST . . . .

DON'T PANIC! Someone will come looking for you soon.

STAY PUT! You can get farther from the trail by wandering around.

BLOW YOUR WHISTLE or shout every once in a while. But don't wear yourself out screaming.

KEEP WARM and DRY.

HURRAH FOR THINGS THAT GROW!

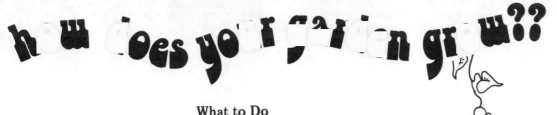

how does your garden grow??

What to Use

- Seeds or seed tapes or seedlings
- Plot of ground
- Tools: shovel or spade for digging
  hoe for making rows
  garden rake
  bucket or hose for watering
  stakes for tomatoes
  strong string
  gloves

What to Do

1. Plan your garden indoors early in the spring. Draw your plan on paper. Make sure you choose things that will grow in your climate.

2. Buy your seeds or seedlings. Read each seed package carefully so that you'll know when and how to plant.

3. Early in the growing season, prepare the soil in your garden. Stake off the area with string. Pull the weeds and turn the soil with a shovel. This part can be hard work. Try to get some friends to help you. The soil needs to be broken up into small pieces until it is loose and crumbly. Make sure you remove any rocks you can pick up.

4. Make the rows and hills that you need for planting. Leave plenty of space between your rows for paths.

5. When you're ready to plant, water the soil well. Follow the directions on each package for planting seeds. Transplant seedlings very carefully.

6. Mark each row so you'll remember what's planted there. You can do this by putting each seed package into a plastic bag and then hanging the bag on a stake at the end of the row.

7. When your plants are tiny, water them often, but do not overwater. As they grow, keep your plants watered often and keep out the weeds!

8. Many plants need to be thinned so the vegetables can grow large. Follow the directions on the package for thinning!

GOOD GARDENING HINTS

* Pay attention to your seed package!

  It will tell you:

  > when to plant
  > how to plant
  > when and how to thin the plants
  > how long the plants take to grow

* Some beans are "climbers." If you plant
  these, put them near a fence.

  Tie strings from the fence to stakes near
  the plants so they can climb.

* Plants such as peppers and tomatoes get a better start indoors.
  You might try growing your seeds inside ahead of time so that
  when the weather is warm, you'll have healthy seedlings started.

* When your tomato plants get about a foot high, tie them to stakes.
  You'll have to tie them again as they grow taller.

* Don't forget to plant your melons and squash and cucumbers
  in little hills.

* Plant your garden in a spot that gets plenty of sun.

* To enrich the soil and keep down the weeds, use your own mulch
  that you've made. (See next page.)

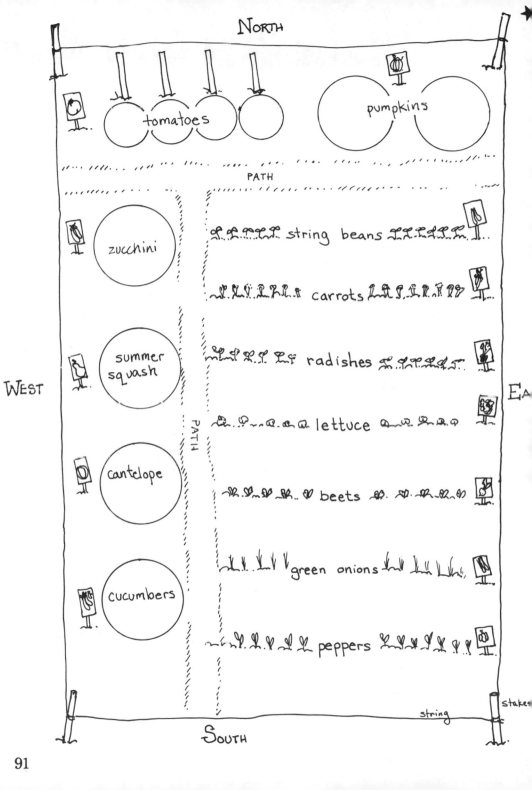

Make Your Own Mulch

Mulch is organic protection for plants. If you spread it around a plant, it will help prevent water evaporation, add nutrients to the soil, protect roots from freezing, and cut down on weed growth that can choke a plant. Here's how you can make your own.

What to Do

1. In the fall, put leaves into the plastic bag until it is about a quarter full.

2. Put in just enough dirt to cover the leaves.

3. Measure out a cup of lime. Pour this into the mixture.

4. Pour in a cup of water.

5. Repeat steps 1, 2, 3, and 4 until you have filled your bag.

6. Tie the bag at the neck with a twist fastener. Lay it out in the sun whenever possible.

7. It's a good idea to give your bag a shake once every other month or so. When you do, untwist the fastener and let a little fresh air in and then reclose the bag tightly.

What to Use

- dry leaves
- water
- dirt
- lime (from a hardware store)
- plastic trash bag

By spring you'll have some fine mulch for your garden.

Every Garden Needs One!

No matter how small your garden is, it surely is a good idea to have a scarecrow to frighten off unwanted visitors! It's even okay to have a tiny scarecrow for your indoor garden!

What to Do

1. Plant one stick firmly into the ground in the center of your garden.

2. Use string to tie the other stick securely across this planted stick at the point where you want the scarecrow's arms to be. Be sure to wrap the string back and forth around all four pieces of pole.

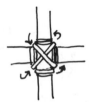

3. Dress the scarecrow with your old clothes. Let some of the clothes flap in the wind so that it looks as if the arms are waving.

4. Attach two strings of small cans or bells to each arm so that they bang together noisily when the wind blows.

What to Use

- 2 sticks or broom handles
- strong string or twine
- old clothes, hat, mittens
- bells or small tin cans

flowers in your garden

What to Use

- seeds or seedlings or seed tapes
- rich soil
- tools: shovel, spade, gloves
- water
- strings and stakes

What to Do

1. Decide where you want to plant flowers. They look wonderful in many different spots—around your vegetable garden, encircling trees, alongside your house, or in a garden all their own.

2. Get the soil ready by turning and loosening and watering it.

3. Read the directions on the packages that tell you when, where, and how to plant the seeds. Transplant seedlings that you've bought or started inside.

4. Tie strings to a fence or to stakes for the plants that are climbers.

5. Keep your plants well watered. (But don't overwater them when they're tiny.) Water the plants by soaking the ground around each plant.

Flowers to try:

petunias	snapdragons
poppies	morning glories
pansies	sweet peas
marigolds	nasturtiums
sunflowers	

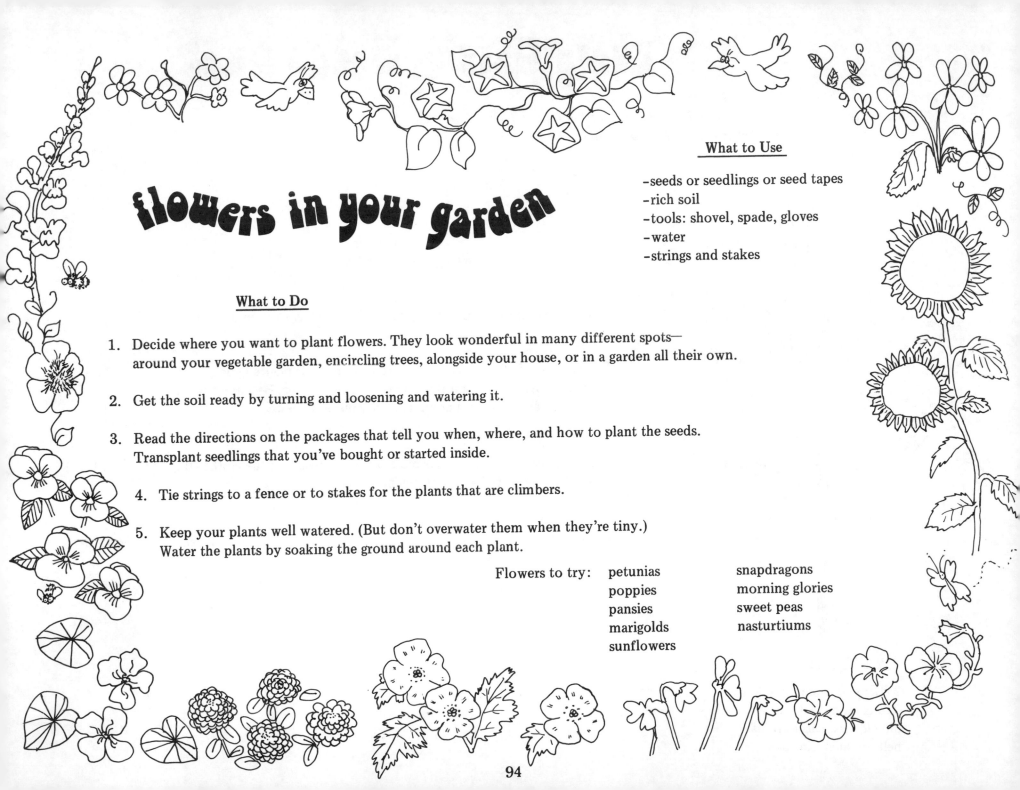

Fall Bulb Planting

What to Use

-BULBS . . .narcissus
        tulips
        iris
        daffodils
        lilies
        amaryllis
        gladiolas
-rich soil
-water

What to Do

1. Early in the fall, buy your bulbs and decide where to plant them. Pay special attention to any directions that come with the bulbs.

2. Turn the ground six inches deep until the soil is fine and loose.

3. Dig holes about five inches deep six–eight inches apart. Plant one bulb in each hole. Cover it with soil.

4. Water the ground well as soon as you have finished planting. Keep it watered if the fall is dry.

5. ENJOY the blooms in spring!!

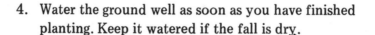

BEWARE!! *There are little critters such as moles and gophers who like to eat bulbs. Cover your bulbs with an old screen or wire mesh if you have such critters around.*

STRAWBERRIES by the barrel!

Wouldn't you like to have a berry-producing barrel in your own backyard? If you get an early spring start, you can be picking and eating your own strawberries by May or June!

What to Use

- old barrel
- strawberry plants
- coarse gravel
- mailing tube
  (2-inch diameter)
- rich soil
- water

What to Do

1. Check country stores or lumber stores to find an inexpensive barrel. (Or use a large wooden box with one end open.)

2. If you have access to a drill, you can make your own holes; otherwise, ask at the store to have holes one inch in diameter drilled about eight inches apart in staggered rows around the barrel.

3. Begin with the barrel in the spot it will call home, because once it is filled with dirt, it will be too heavy to be moved.

4. Spread a two-inch layer of coarse gravel over the bottom of the barrel.

5. Put the mailing tube upright in the center of the barrel and fill the tube with gravel. (The gravel will provide an easy path for water on its way to thirsty roots!)

6. Keeping the mailing tube in place, begin filling the barrel with rich soil.

7. When the soil reaches the level of the first holes, tuck the roots of a single plant into each hole.

8. Water (to pack and settle the soil) as you go along, adding plants and soil until you've reached the top of the barrel. Make sure the roots of the plants are under the soil and the tops of the plants are not!

9. Finish by finding spots for a few more plants on the top.

10. Pull the mailing tube out from around the gravel.

Hints for a happier harvest:

1. *Use June-bearing strawberries rather than an everbearing variety.*

2. *Since strawberries are usually small the first year, pinch back most of the blossoms and enjoy bigger, better berries the second time around!*

3. *If winters aren't mild in your area, take care to protect your barrel from very cold temperatures by covering it with a plastic cover or a heavy mulch.*

An Inside Arbor

*You can bring a cool, green arbor into your very own room!
Imagine sleeping under green leaves—it's almost like camping
out-of-doors! It's easy to do, makes very little mess—and it gives you
something delightful to watch as it continues to grow each day.*

What to Use

- any leafy vine plant
  (potato, bean, etc.)
- string
- thumbtacks

What to Do

1. First, show this idea to a grown-up and ask permission
   to put some thumbtacks in your wall.

2. Buy some vine plants in containers, or grow your
   own from a sweet potato or bean seedling.

3. Put the plants in your room around your bed.

*If it isn't a good idea to grow
your arbor inside (and lots of times it isn't),
choose a small area outside. Drive a stake
as tall as you are into the ground and plant
your vines in a circle around it. After the vines
begin to grow, attach strings from the stake to
each plant, and you'll have an outside arbor
very soon!*

4. Tie one end of a long piece of string around the plant's
   container. Securely thumbtack the other end of the
   string to the wall at the head or side of your bed, or
   around your desk. The more plants you use, the larger
   your arbor will be.

5. Watch your vines grow! Once the vines are long enough, gently wrap them around the strings. They will automatically continue to wrap themselves around the strings and move forward as they grow. Soon they will cover the entire length of the string, and you'll have a wonderful hide-out that will last for a long time.

6. Be sure to water and care for your plants.

A Great Growing Trick

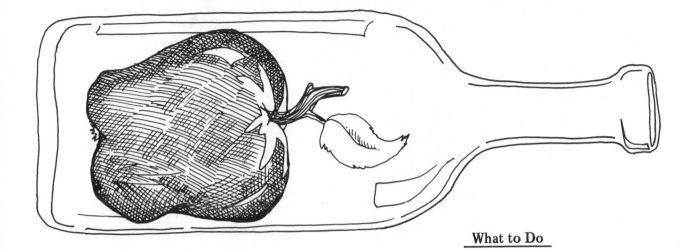

What to Use

-fruit tree (or cucumber or zucchini plant)
-some strong string
-long jar or bottle with a narrow neck

What to Do

1. Early in the growing season, when fruit trees have very tiny fruit or when the cucumber and zucchini plants have tiny vegetables, choose a small apple or peach or pear or cucumber or zucchini for your trick.

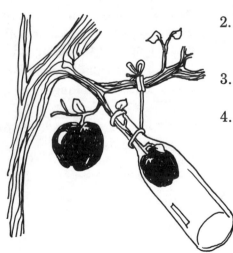

2. Very gently, place the part of the branch or vine holding the small fruit or vegetable through the neck into the bottle.

3. Carefully tie the bottle to a strong branch of the tree (or lay it on the ground in the vegetable patch).

4. The bottle will act as a hothouse, particularly if you have chosen a sunny spot. Keep watching as the fruit or vegetable grows. When it is large enough to fill the jar, cut it from the vine or tree.

5. See if your friends can guess how you ever got the fruit or vegetable through that skinny neck into the bottle!!

ready, set, GROW!

What to Use

- pumpkin seeds
- garden plot
- plenty of water
- several kids

*Hey, try this contest with watermelons
or zucchinis or cucumbers or tomatoes!!*

What to Do

1. Enlist a bunch of friends to be in on your Great Pumpkin Race! Give each pumpkin farmer the same number of seeds (4-6).

2. Everyone must plant all the seeds on the same day. Choose a starting day and an ending day. The seed package will give you an idea of how many days the growing takes.

3. Each farmer should plant his/her seeds in his/her own hill. (Make sure there is plenty of space between hills.) Then everyone is responsible for the watering, weeding, and care of his/her own plants. As they appear, the smallest pumpkins should be picked off the vines to allow all the growing energy to go into the biggest pumpkins.

4. On the ending date, all pumpkins should be weighed and measured to find the winner. You might want to give prizes for the heaviest, the fattest, the tallest, the orangest, the most unusual shape.

5. WHAT NEXT?? Why, gigantic jack-o-lanterns, of course!!

Parsley Planter

What to Use

- egg carton
- broken eggshells
- small pieces of sponge
- parsley seeds
- water

Parsley tastes good all by itself, and makes a delicious dish look even prettier when sprigs of it are added around the food. Make sure your home has a constant supply of it by growing your own.

What to Do

1. Put half an eggshell in each pocket of the egg carton.

2. Cut a piece of sponge to fit in each shell.

3. Wet the sponge pieces.

4. Sprinkle parsley seeds on the sponges.

5. Water the seeds a little every day.

6. Watch your plants closely. In about a week, the sprouts will start to show. Let them grow, and when you're ready to eat them, snip some with a scissors.

This egg carton garden will grow watercress and grass, too. Ask someone at a garden supply store what other plants you could try.

CACTUS GARDEN

What to Use

- small cacti
- shallow bowl
- sand
- small stones and pebbles
- pieces of driftwood, bark or tree branch
- water

What to Do

1. Purchase two or three cacti at a plant store.

2. Sprinkle a few small pebbles in the bottom of the bowl. Fill the bowl with sand.

3. Plant the cactus plants.

4. Add the wood pieces, small rocks and pebbles to the arrangement.

5. Sprinkle the whole arrangement with water and place on a window sill.

CAUTION: Do not over-water your cactus garden. Remember that cactus is a desert plant not accustomed to much moisture.

Pot Your Plants Creatively

What to Use

–½ gallon milk carton
–straw placemat
–scissors
–glue
–yarn or felt
–plant
–soil

What to Do

1. Cut the top off the milk container. Wash and dry the container.

2. Wrap the placemat around the container and cut it to fit. Mesh the edges carefully and glue them into place.

3. Cut decorative shapes from the felt and glue them on, or make designs with the yarn and glue them in place. (Don't use too much decoration as you want the plant to be the main attraction.)

4. Fill the pot with good, rich soil and add the plant. Water carefully.

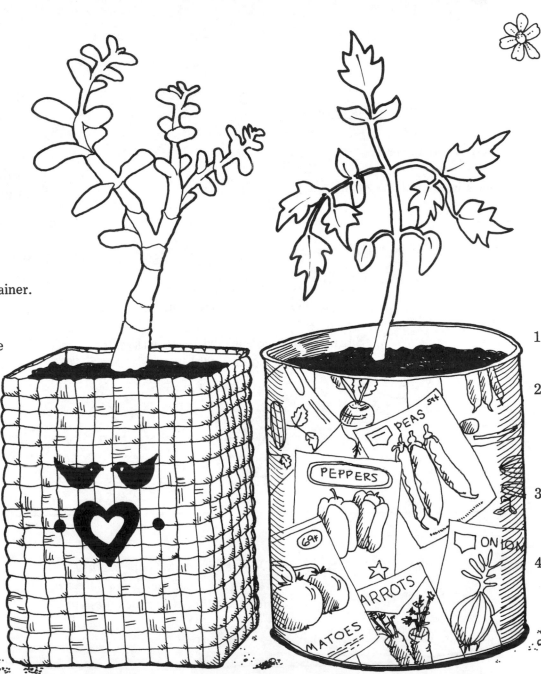

What to Use

–coffee can
–seeds
–seed packages
–glue
–scissors
–shellac
–brush
–soil

What to Do

1. Wash and dry the coffee can.

2. Arrange the seed packages to form an interesting design. (Trim with the scissors to fit the can.) Glue in place.

3. Cover the can with a coat of clear shellac for protection.

4. Fill with soil and plant tomato, pepper or parsley seeds.

What to Use

- ½ pint milk cartons
- scissors
- brown paper bag
- popsicle sticks
- glue
- yarn, rick-rack or cord
- a blooming plant
- soil

What to Use

- old clay or plastic flower pots
- cotton fabric
- scissors
- glue
- plants
- soil

What to Do

1. Cut the top off the milk carton, then wash and dry the milk carton thoroughly.

2. Cut the brown paper bag to fit. Glue it to the milk carton.

3. Arrange popsicle sticks around the sides, fence-like. Glue them in place.

4. Tie the yarn, rick-rack or cord around the outside and tie a flat bow or two.

5. Fill with soil and add one blooming plant. A marigold or a pansy grows well in a container of this size.

What to Do

1. Wash and dry the flower pots to remove all old dirt.

2. Cut the fabric to completely cover the pot. (Patchwork design or calico is nice.)

3. Use lots of glue to stick the fabric in place.

4. Allow the glue to dry overnight before filling with soil.

5. Add ivy or philodendron plants to the pots.

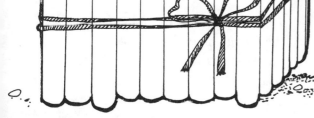

What to Do

1. Wash and dry your bottle.

2. Cut several lengths of the yarn.

3. Wrap one piece of yarn around the container at a time. Add dabs of glue here and there.

4. Wrap a different color of yarn around each time to get a rainbow effect.

5. Continue wrapping and adding glue until the bottle is covered.

6. Add water and cuttings from other plants.

What to Use

- empty bottle (cooking oil, wine, or salad dressing bottle)
- glue
- scissors
- different colored yarn scraps
- cuttings from plants
- water

What to Use

- styrofoam coffee cups (heaviest grade you can get)
- green construction paper
- scissors
- glue
- soil
- shamrock plant or clover

What to Do

1. Cut out four-leaf clover designs from the green paper.

2. Glue these all over the cup.

3. Fill the cup with soil and plant one shamrock plant or a clump of clover.

These cups won't last long, but they make nice place cards, or use them in a grouping for a St. Patrick's Day table setting.

What to Do

1. Wash and dry the container.

2. Paint the outside of the container in a bright, sunny color.

3. Glue buttons, beads, shells, or pebbles all over the container. To get an interesting mix of colors and textures, use the larger items first and fill in gaps with smaller ones.

4. Allow the pot to dry overnight before filling with soil and adding small plants.

What to Use

- cottage cheese or ice cream containers
- tempera or poster paint
- brush
- buttons, beads, shells, small pebbles, etc.
- glue
- soil
- small plants

What to Do

1. Arrange the clothespins all around the basket in the most interesting design you can create.

2. Glue clothespins in place and allow the glue to dry.

3. Slip a potted plant that needs a new home into the basket—pot and all!

What to Use

- old basket
- glue
- wooden clothespins
- a potted plant

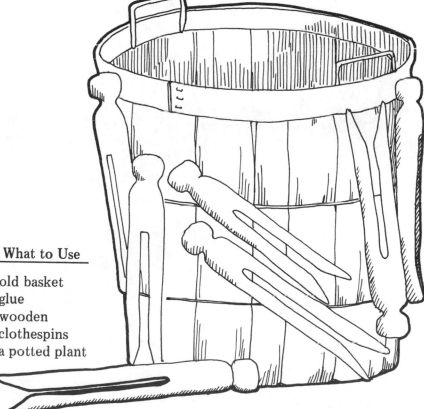

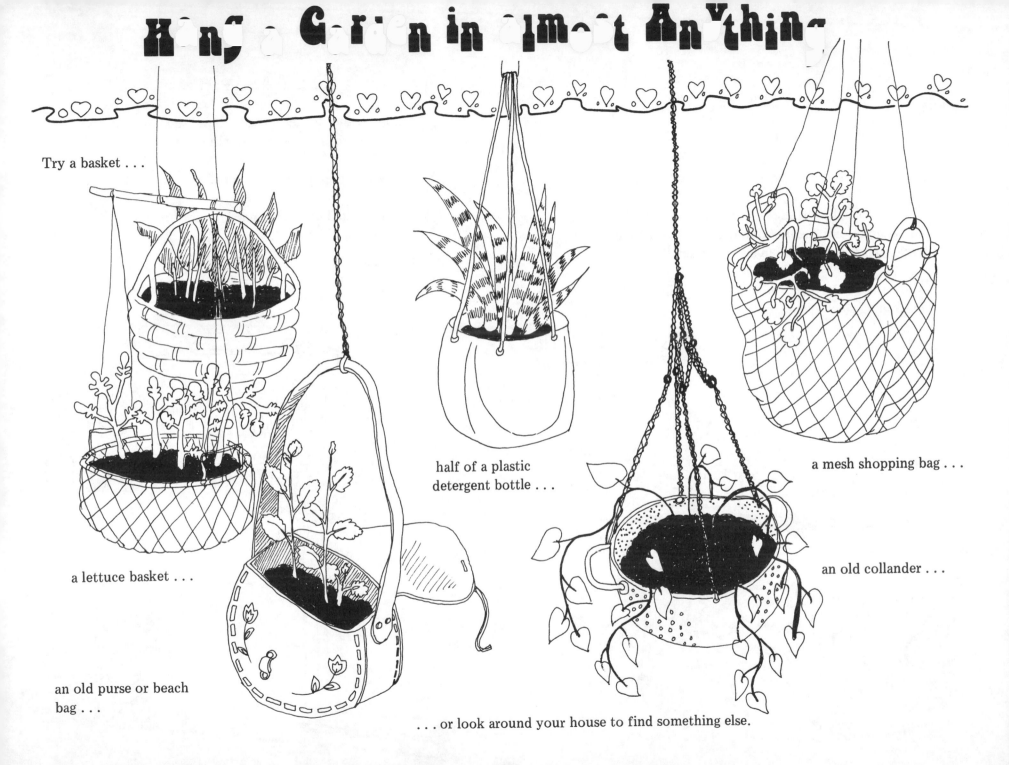

Hang a Garden in Almost Anything

Try a basket . . .

a lettuce basket . . .

an old purse or beach bag . . .

half of a plastic detergent bottle . . .

an old collander . . .

a mesh shopping bag . . .

. . . or look around your house to find something else.

What to Do

1. Buy a package of sphagnum moss at a garden center or dime store. Take it home and soak it in a container of water until it is completely saturated. (This will take several hours, so be patient!)

2. While the moss is soaking, select a container for your garden and clean it thoroughly. If there are no holes in the container, ask an adult to help you use an ice pick to punch a few in the bottom so the finished planter will be able to drain. Also, punch three holes at equal distances around the top of the container. You'll attach your hanger there.

3. To make your garden hang, you'll need to braid some cord. Decide how high you want your basket to hang, and cut three pieces of cord that length. Securely knot one end of each cord and thread each through one of the three holes you punched near the top of your container. Leave plenty of room for the plant, and then bring the three strands together and braid. Tie off the top ends into a knot, and make a loop for hanging.

4. Now, carefully squeeze the excess water out of the moss. Make a lining of it at least two inches thick for the bottom of the container and at least one inch thick for the sides.

What to Use

- container
- ice pick
- sphagnum moss
- water
- soil
- cord or heavy yarn
- plants, seeds or seedlings

5. Add a good soil mixture on top of the moss, and your garden is ready to be planted.

6. A crop of mini-vegetables would be good to hang in the kitchen. Try planting squash, cucumbers, or radishes. Watercress, mint, or parsley would be nice to have around, too.

7. Hang your garden in a sunny window and water it about once a week. (Follow the directions on your seed packages.) Remember to put a bowl under the garden to catch the water when it drips. The moss should absorb most of it, but don't take any chances!

Don't Throw Away the Seeds!

What to Do

1. Remove pumpkin seeds from your pumpkins, or sunflower seeds from the heads of "dead" sunflowers.

2. Clean the pumpkin seeds well and salt them a little.

3. Soak the sunflower seeds overnight in saltwater.

4. Dry the seeds well.

5. Spread seeds out on a cookie sheet that has been lightly oiled. Bake in a low oven (200°) for ½ hour–1 hour or until crisp and a little browned.

    OR

    Fry in a lightly oiled frying pan, stirring the seeds often. They're ready when they look browned or crisp.

6. Let the seeds cool. Then they're ready to eat!

If you don't wish to eat the seeds, try planting them again (uncooked) OR feed them to the birds!!

What to Use

- pumpkin or sunflower seeds
- cooking oil
- salt
- frying pan or oven
- adult help

HUG A TREE

Each tree is a special, individual living thing—just as each person is. Here's a game you can play that will help you get to know one tree individually!

What to Do

1. Walk through a forest (or park or yard) and choose one tree—any tree you like!

2. Close your eyes and hug the tree.
   How big is it? Can you reach around it?

3. Keep your eyes closed. Run your hands up and down the tree.
   How does the bark feel on your hands?
   Can you feel any sap?
   Touch the leaves or needles. How do they feel?

4. Keep your eyes closed. Press your cheek against the tree.
   How does it feel?
   Is it rough? smooth? uneven? even?
   Is the bark thick or thin?

5. Keep your eyes closed and sniff the tree.
   How does it smell?
   What does the smell remind you of?
   Smell the sap, needles, leaves, bark.

6. Press your ear against the tree.
   Can you hear its heartbeat? (The heartbeat is best heard in spring with a stethescope.)
   What other sounds does the tree make?

7. Open your eyes and look at the tree from top to bottom.
   Is it alive or dead?
   Is it straight or crooked?
   Can you count the branches?
   Does it have leaves? needles? cones? blossoms? nuts?
   Who are its neighbors?
   Who lives in the tree?
   How old do you think it is?
   Can you see any roots?

What to Use

- a tree
- yourself

If you can climb the tree, DO. Sit up there and look around to see how the world looks to your tree.
What has this tree seen in its life?
What does the tree know?

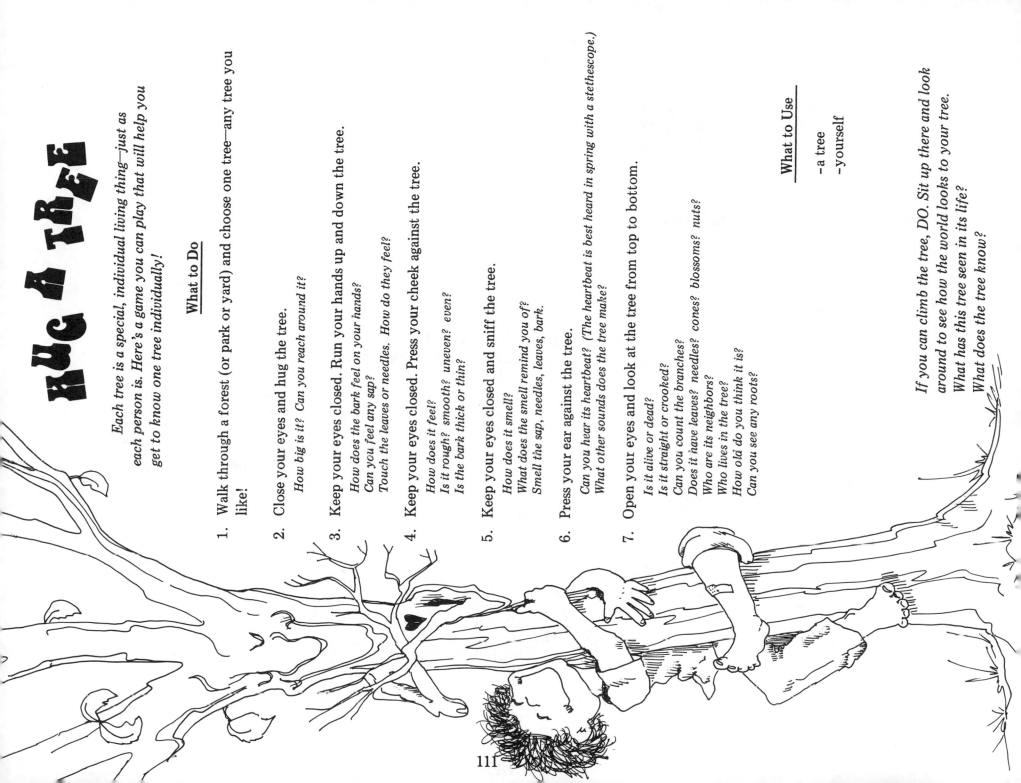

111

Leaf People

What to Do

1. Arrange leaves on the sheet of paper to make bodies for leaf people.

2. Glue the leaves in place.

3. Add a head, legs, and arms with markers.
   (Some smaller leaves may be used for hats, boots, etc.)

4. Use your imagination to make creatures from outer space, ladies in fancy gowns, a character from your favorite TV show or replicas of people you know.

What to Use

- leaves
- white glue
- paper
- markers

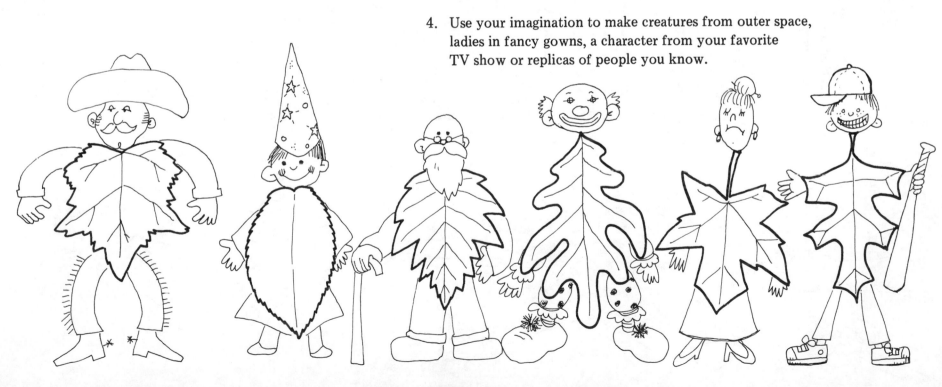

112

stained glass leaf collage

What to Use

- 2 sheets of waxed paper
  cut to fit a pane in your window
- leaves of all kinds
- crayons (assorted colors)
- crayon sharpener (a dull butter
  knife is a good substitute)
- thin towel
- an iron
- adult help

What to Do

1. Collect all kinds of leaves and other flat growing things.

2. Arrange your leaves the way you want them on one of the sheets of waxed paper.

3. Peel the paper covers from your crayons and scrape or sharpen them so that the shavings fall on top of the leaves.

4. Put the second piece of waxed paper over this.

5. Heat your iron to medium, lay a thin towel over the waxed paper, and carefully press. The heat from the iron will melt the crayon shavings and wax to hold your creation together.

6. Let your collage cool. Then tape it to your window, and you've made your own stained glass!

Nature Rubbings

- crayons
- tissue or rice paper
- ferns or leaves
- newspapers
- masking tape
- construction paper

What to Do

1. Collect fern fronds or leaves to be rubbed.

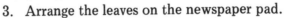

2. Place a flat stack of old newspapers on a flat work surface to make a pad for your rubbing.

3. Arrange the leaves on the newspaper pad.

4. Place the paper over the arrangement and secure it with masking tape.

5. Select the color of crayon you want to use and rub its flat side over the paper.

6. Use a contrasting color of construction paper to make a frame for the rubbing.

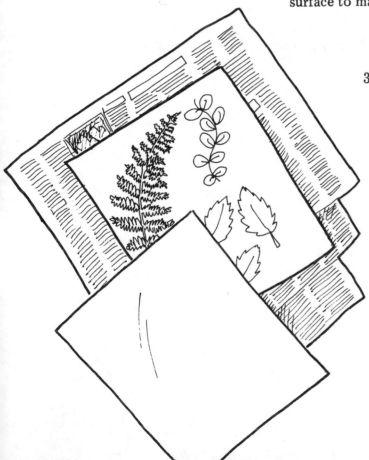

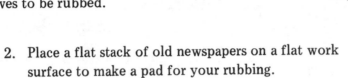

will daisies tell...?

An old legend has it that you can test the trueness of your true love's love by pulling the petals from a daisy. Beginning with the first petal you say, "He(She) loves me," the second, "He(She) loves me not," and so on till the last petal gives you the message. Try it—What will the answer be? Does he/she love you?

If you can't find daisies, use clovers or any sweet-smelling long-stemmed flower.

1. Pick as many daisies as you need with stems as long as possible.

2. Make a slit in each stem. (See illustration.)

3. Thread the daisies together by pulling one stem through the other until you have a chain as long as you need.

4. Use the chain to make a jump rope, belt, crown or some other very special daisy doodad.

TOADSTOOL TRACKS

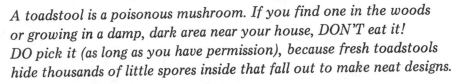

A toadstool is a poisonous mushroom. If you find one in the woods or growing in a damp, dark area near your house, DON'T eat it! DO pick it (as long as you have permission), because fresh toadstools hide thousands of little spores inside that fall out to make neat designs.

What to Use

- toadstool
- liquid white glue
- water
- brush
- plastic or paper cup
- mounting paper
- two pencils
- bowl
- hair spray

What to Do

1. Find a toadstool or get a fresh mushroom from the grocery store. Make sure that the cap has not been broken away from the stem.

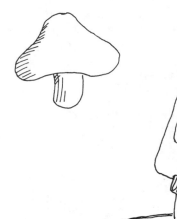

2. Put some glue into the plastic cup. Add just a little water to thin the glue, then stir.

3. Cut the stem off the toadstool, or move it around very carefully with your fingers to separate it from the cap. If a good deal of the toadstool's underside is covered by the rim, carefully trim away enough rim so that the spores can fall out.

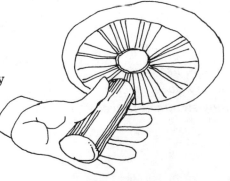

116

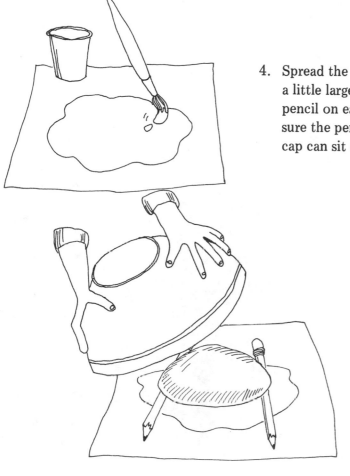

4. Spread the glue mixture on the paper in a circle a little larger than the toadstool cap. Put one pencil on each side of the circle of glue. Make sure the pencils are close enough so the toadstool cap can sit on them.

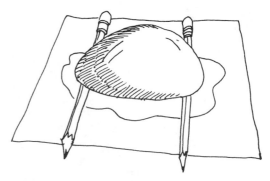

5. Place the cap on the two pencils over the circle of glue.

6. Cover the toadstool with a bowl. Be careful not to disturb anything as you put the bowl down. Leave the bowl in place for at least 24 hours.

7. Lift the bowl off, then gently take the toadstool cap and pencils away. You'll find an intricate design made by the toadstool spores embedded in your glue mixture!

8. When your design is dry, spray it with hair spray to protect it.

AW SHUCKS!

Gather corn shucks from a field (or save them from your summer corn). You can make them into dolls to decorate your Christmas tree, make miniature scenes or add to autumn centerpieces.

OR

You can start your own collection of original dolls. Make some new ones each year to add to the collection. Try to create lots of different characters.

What to Use

- dried corn shucks
- corn silks
- fine point colored markers
- "strings" made from shucks
- scissors

What to Do

1. Use corn shucks that are good and dry. Cut the shucks carefully away from the woody base.

2. Soak the shucks in warm water to make them pliable.

3. Slit some shucks with scissors to make strips for use in tying the dolls (or use plastic string).

4. Fold several long, strong husks in the middle. Tie a strip around the husks near the fold to make a head.

5. Beneath the tied strip, insert two or three smaller husks between the folded husks for arms. Tie another strip below the arms.

6. Shape the bottom half into a long dress or legs.

7. Use braided corn silk to make hair and weave it into the shucks.

8. Draw facial features with colored markers.

9. Small pieces of shucks may be used to make a purse, a suitcase, books, buttons, bows, an umbrella, a golf club, etc.

Give each of your dolls a personality all its own!!

Decorations for your Door

Someone's sure to be knocking at your door . . . if it's decorated with a bicycle basket filled with dried flowers and/or grasses.

Add a pretty bow for that extra touch!

If you don't have a basket, just tie a sheaf of grasses and weeds together with velvet ribbon or calico.

If you have a selection of shells, string together a whole cluster with braided or corded yarn, and make a loop for hanging. Just for fun, you could tuck in some bells between the shells. (The kind you buy at the five-and-ten-cent store at Christmas time are great—you get a whole card full—so the more, the merrier!!)

Fringe a strip of burlap on both sides and hang it between two dowels to make a bright door banner of some selected sand dollars, sea horses or oyster shells. Add some pieces of seaweed for interest.

Make a wreath by weaving dried or straw flowers into a circle and tying on a checked gingham bow!

If you prefer something a little fancier, you might string gourds, okra or cockle-bur pods, pine cones, thistles and nuts together to make a door garland.

A BOUQUET TO LAST

It's easy to bring spring indoors when flowers are in bloom. But wouldn't you love some flower freshness to brighten up a cold winter day? Here's how.

What to Use

- garden flowers (Ask
  permission before you pick!)
- string
- wire hanger
- scissors
- vase

What to Do

1. Pick a big bouquet of flowers. Leave the stems long, but pull off all the leaves.

2. Use the string to tie the flower stems together tightly.

3. Tie the bouquet to a wire hanger. The bouquet should hang upside down.

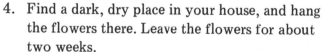

4. Find a dark, dry place in your house, and hang the flowers there. Leave the flowers for about two weeks.

5. Untie your flowers, and arrange them in a vase. Put them in your room or in the middle of the kitchen table for the whole family to enjoy.

These will last for many months!

how to DRY flowers, leaves, & grasses

What to Use

- cornmeal
- borax
- long, shallow box with top
- clean paint brush
- leaves, flowers, grasses

What to Do

1. Mix equal parts of cornmeal and borax.

2. Spread a one-inch layer of the mixture in the bottom of the box.

3. Spread flowers, leaves or grasses out on the mixture.

4. Sprinkle more of the mixture on top of the flowers to cover them.

5. Put the top on the box and set it in a dry place for about three weeks.

6. Take the dried plants out of the mixture and brush the dust off with the paint brush.

124

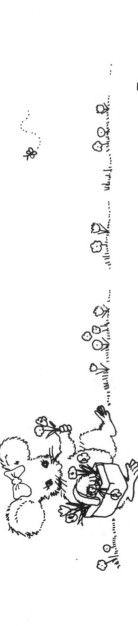

how to
STORE dried flowers, leaves, & grasses

Tiny, thin flowers and grasses such as violets, lillies of the valley, or honeysuckle can be pressed in a thick, mail-order catalog or a telephone directory. Just be sure to leave plenty of pages between each waxed-paper-wrapped flower, and to put the bricks on top. That weight is important.

And always store your drying flowers, leaves or grasses in a dry place.

What to Use

- cigar box, candy box or shoe box
- tweezers
- tissue paper or paper napkins

What to Do

1. Remove the waxed-paper-wrapped materials from the flower press.

2. Check to see if any of the petals or ends are out of shape or mashed. If they are, use the tweezers to straighten them as best you can. Handle very carefully.

3. Store them in the box, one layer at a time, with paper protectors between each layer.

how to PRESS flowers, leaves, & grasses

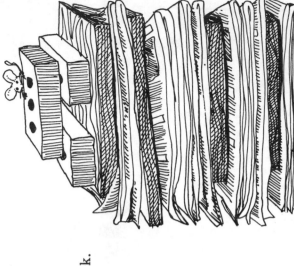

What to Use

- old book
- waxed paper
- newspapers
- flat boards
- bricks
- scissors

What to Do

1. Cut and fold waxed paper in half (to fit inside the pages of your book) to take along with you on your search for flowers, leaves and grasses.

2. As you pick each one, slip it between the folded pieces of waxed paper. This will protect the tiny details and avoid shattered petals and broken ends.

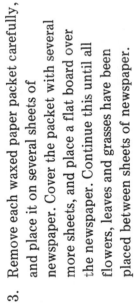

3. Remove each waxed paper packet carefully, and place it on several sheets of newspaper. Cover the packet with several more sheets, and place a flat board over the newspaper. Continue this until all flowers, leaves and grasses have been placed between sheets of newspaper.

4. Put bricks on top of the whole stack. Leave the stack for several weeks without disturbing it.

126

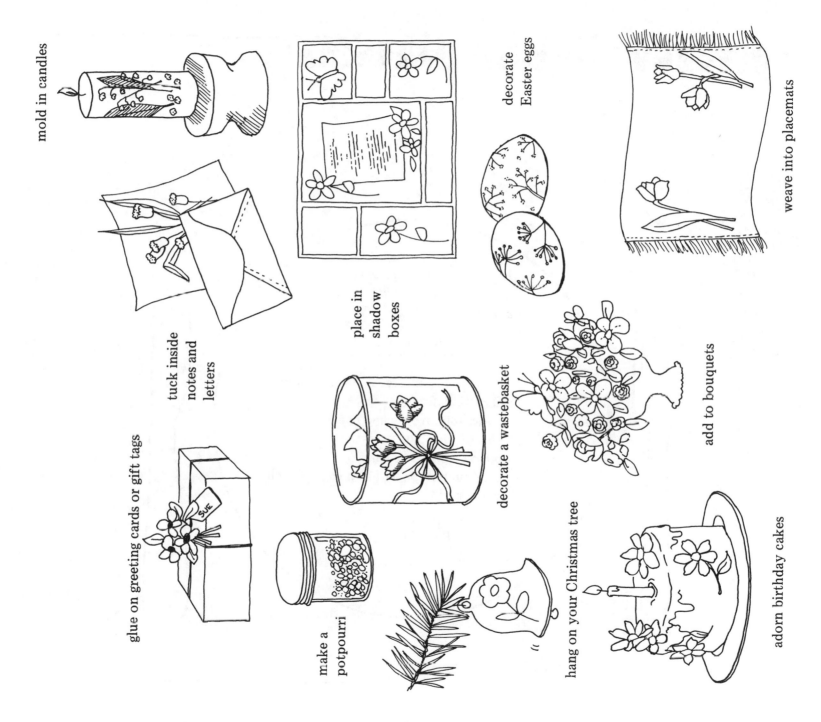

You can use pressed and dried flowers, leaves and grasses from your collection all year long to

mold in candles

tuck inside notes and letters

place in shadow boxes

decorate Easter eggs

weave into placemats

glue on greeting cards or gift tags

make a potpourri

decorate a wastebasket

add to bouquets

hang on your Christmas tree

adorn birthday cakes

127

pressed flower placemats

Here's the perfect present for a nature lover who likes to set a naturally beautiful table!

What to Use

- pressed flowers (see Pressed Flower Directions)
- clear, adhesive-backed paper
- clear drying glue
- plain tagboard or heavy construction paper (12-inch x 18-inch)
- scissors
- ruler
- straight pin

What to Do

1. Decide what color and texture you want your placemats to be.
   Buy enough paper to make at least four 12-inch x 18-inch mats.
   (If you are making mats for a family, be sure to make at least one
   more mat than there are family members so a guest could use one, too.)

2. Cut your paper to the proper size. You may want to ruffle or tear
   the edges or use pinking shears to make pretty borders.

3. Cut two pieces of the adhesive-backed paper for each mat
   (this will waterproof them and make them easy to clean).
   Make sure the clear paper extends about ½-inch from all edges
   of the mat. Attach a piece of paper to the back of <u>each</u> mat.

4. Place a few pressed flowers on one of the sheets of paper, and
   move them around until you make a design you like. Glue
   the flowers in place and set them aside to dry. Follow this same
   procedure for each mat.

5. Very carefully attach the second piece of clear paper to the front
   of the mat. If little bubbles appear when you do this, prick them
   with a straight pin and smooth out. You may also need to trim
   the edges to make them even.

6. Wrap the set of mats in tissue paper and tie a bow
   around them. Put another sprig of dried flowers
   through your bow, and your gift is ready!

NATURE NOTES

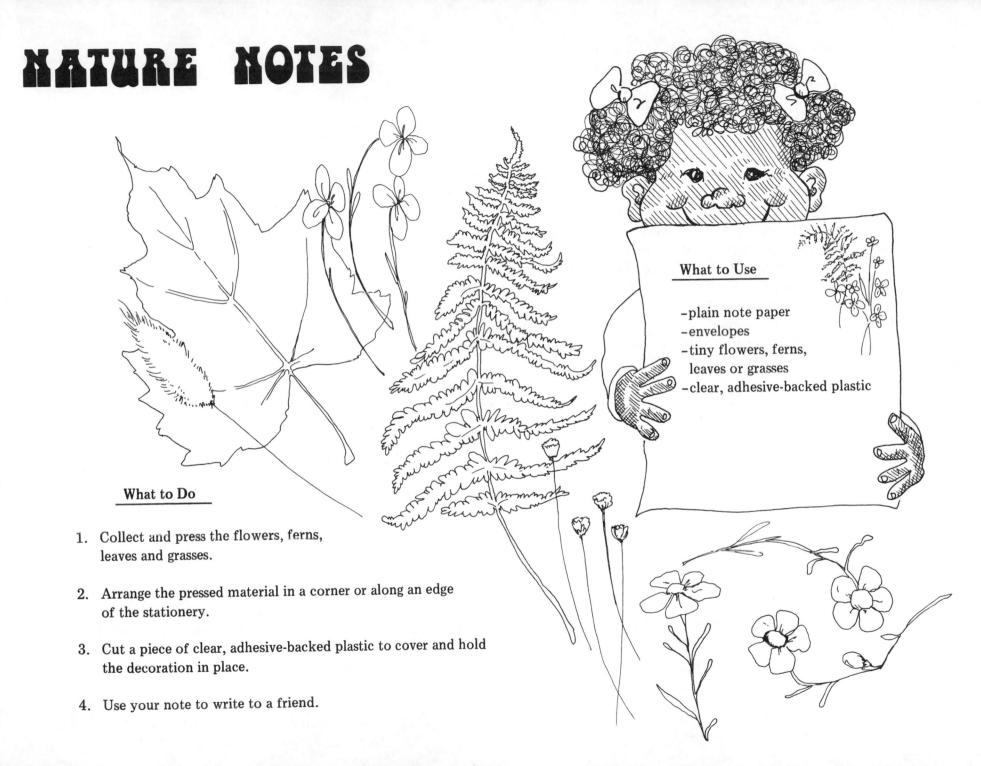

What to Use

- plain note paper
- envelopes
- tiny flowers, ferns, leaves or grasses
- clear, adhesive-backed plastic

What to Do

1. Collect and press the flowers, ferns, leaves and grasses.

2. Arrange the pressed material in a corner or along an edge of the stationery.

3. Cut a piece of clear, adhesive-backed plastic to cover and hold the decoration in place.

4. Use your note to write to a friend.

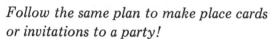

Follow the same plan to make place cards or invitations to a party!

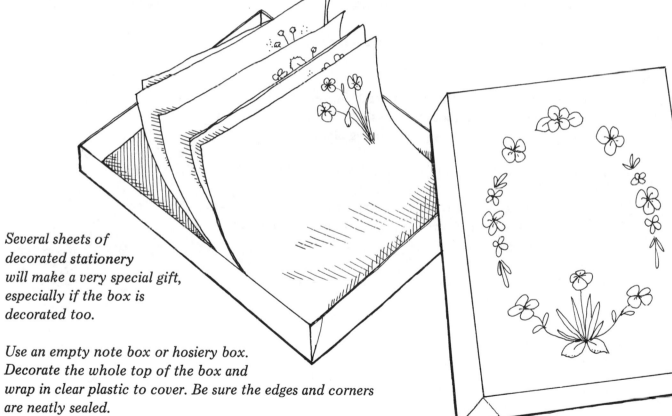

Several sheets of decorated stationery will make a very special gift, especially if the box is decorated too.

Use an empty note box or hosiery box. Decorate the whole top of the box and wrap in clear plastic to cover. Be sure the edges and corners are neatly sealed.

Dried Flower Bookmarks

What to Do

1. Gather some small flowers early in the morning when they are freshest.

2. Put a thin layer of sand in the bottom of the pie pan.

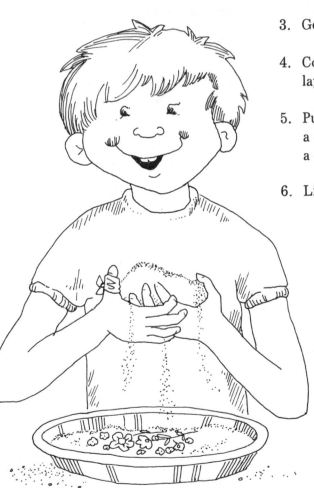

3. Gently place the flowers on top of the sand.

4. Completely cover the flowers with another layer of sand.

5. Put the pie pan with the sand-covered flowers in a dark, dry spot for about ten days. (An attic or a dark closet will make a good "hiding place.")

6. Lift the flowers out and gently brush the sand off.

7. Cut a strip of construction paper to form a bookmark. Arrange the flowers attractively and glue them to the paper.

8. Cover the whole strip with adhesive-backed clear plastic.

What to Use

- small flowers (violets, baby's breath, lily of the valley, sweet william, etc.)
- foil pie pan
- sand
- scissors (pinking shears if you have them)
- construction paper
- adhesive-backed clear plastic

132

Flowers under Glass

What to Do

1. Select a color and texture of background cloth that will show off your dried flower arrangement in the best way possible. Velvet and felt are nice for dainty arrangements, while corduroy and burlap compliment heavier ones.

2. Cut the fabric the same size as the cardboard backing.

3. Glue the fabric to the cardboard and allow to dry.

4. Arrange the flowers and grasses on the fabric. Use the tweezers to spread petals and strands apart.

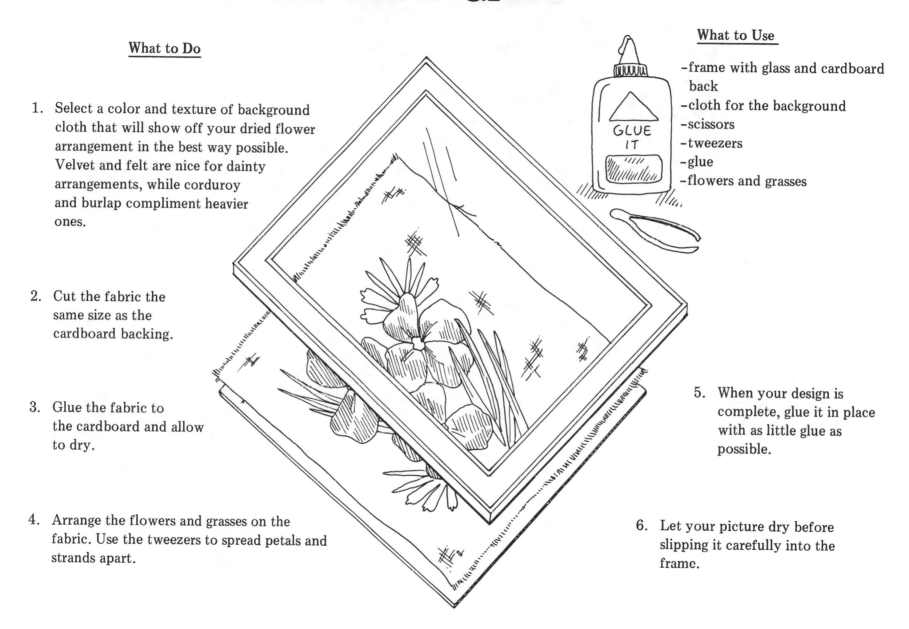

What to Use

- frame with glass and cardboard back
- cloth for the background
- scissors
- tweezers
- glue
- flowers and grasses

5. When your design is complete, glue it in place with as little glue as possible.

6. Let your picture dry before slipping it carefully into the frame.

BLOOMING CANDLES

What to Use

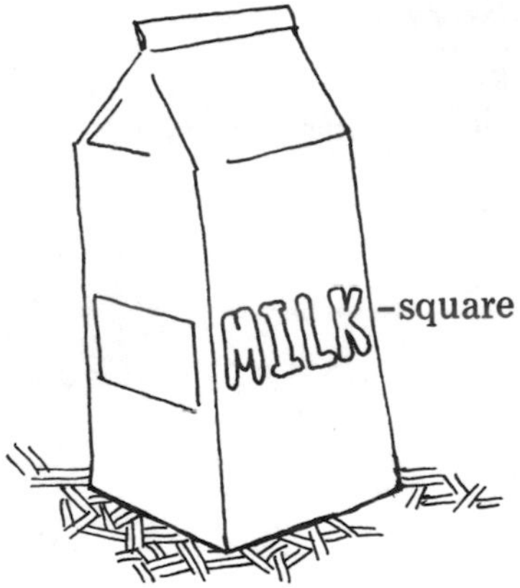

-square milk carton

-cooking oil or margarine

-parrafin

-old candle

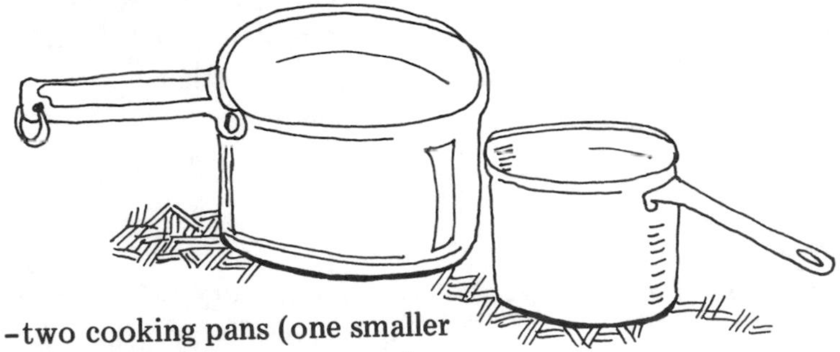

-two cooking pans (one smaller
than the other), a stove and
hot pads

-tuna fish can

-double stick tape

-pressed flowers with stems (larkspurs,
black-eyed susans and goldenrod
are good choices)

*CAUTION: Candlemaking with hot wax must be done carefully.
Ask a grownup to help you.*

1. Select a milk carton the size you want your candle to be.
    Cut the top part off and make a smooth edge.

2. Wash and dry the carton. Grease the bottom and sides
    with cooking oil or margarine.

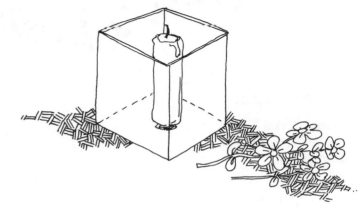

3. Tape the candle to the bottom of the carton
    to make it stand up straight.

4. Make a double boiler by setting the tuna fish can
    inside the large pan, surrounding it with water,
    and putting the smaller pan on top of the can.

5. Put the paraffin in the small pan.

6. Set the whole pan stack on a stove burner turned on medium
    and melt the parrafin. (You may need a grownup to help you do this.)

7. Carefully place a flower spray in the carton.

8. Pour the melted parrafin in the carton, making sure
    the flower spray and candle stay in place.
    Leave the parrafin to harden overnight.

9. Carefully peel away the carton to see your
    blooming candle!

flowers to eat???

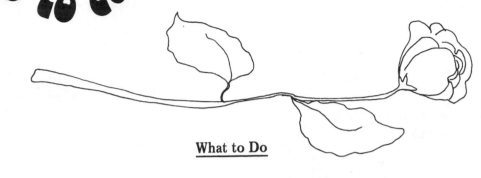

What to Use

- rose petals
- violet or nasturtium blossoms
- 1 egg white
- ½ cup sugar
- paper towels
- egg beater
- small bowl

What to Do

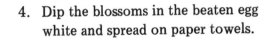

1. Pick flowers to be used early in the morning before the sun has wilted them. Violet and nasturtium blossoms are lightweight, so the whole flower may be used. Roses are too heavy, so they need to be separated into individual petals.

2. Wash the blossoms very carefully, and shake off all extra water. Place on paper towels to dry.

3. Put the egg white in the bowl and beat until stiff and frothy.

4. Dip the blossoms in the beaten egg white and spread on paper towels.

5. Sprinkle sugar evenly all over the blossoms. (Use plenty of sugar.) Let dry before shaking off the extra.

6. Use to decorate cakes, cupcakes or ice cream balls for a very special occasion.

Hurrah For Daytime & Nighttime Skies!

Sun Time Silhouettes

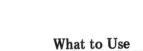

What to Do

1. Find a friend to trace around your shadow.

2. Place the paper in very strong sunlight, then stand so your profile falls on the white paper.

3. Have your friend trace your profile with a pencil.

4. Cut out the profile and mount it on black construction paper.

Blueprints in Broad Daylight

What to Use

- dark blue paper
- tape
- scissors
- objects for printing
  (leaves, petals, thick grasses)
- sunshine

What to Do

1. Lay out leaves, shells, grasses or other natural objects in an interesting arrangement on the blue paper.

2. Make tiny rolls of tape. Use these to lightly tape each item to the paper. Use the tape on the edges of the items so that no sunshine sneaks under them. Do not let any of the tape show.

3. Lay the paper in strong sunshine on a sidewalk or table. Tape the paper down so that it doesn't blow away.

4. Leave the paper in the sun all day. Take the materials off carefully at the end of the day.

NOTE: If the paper hasn't faded enough on the first day, you might leave the objects on and put the paper out for more fading on another sunny day!

Sunshine & Shadows

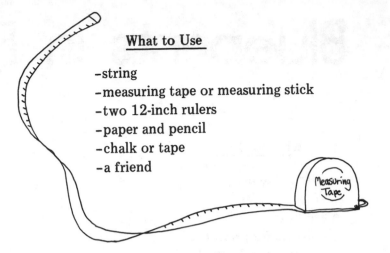

What to Use

- string
- measuring tape or measuring stick
- two 12-inch rulers
- paper and pencil
- chalk or tape
- a friend

What to Do

1. On a sunny day, have a friend measure your shadow early in the morning. Use a measuring stick or tape to do the measuring, or make a mark on the ground with tape or chalk.

2. Stand in the same spot at noon and get your shadow measured again.

3. Have another measurement taken late in the afternoon and another before sundown. Keep a record of all the measurements.

What's happening to your shadow???

Try measuring shadows of other things during the day, too (stop signs, bushes, houses, etc.).

*You can also use shadows to find out the height of very tall things,
such as buildings and trees.*

What to Do

1. Guess the height of your tree (or a house or swing set). Write down your guess.

2. Hold one ruler straight up next to the tree. Use the other ruler to measure the first ruler's shadow. Write down the measurement.

3. Now measure the shadow of the tree. Write down the measurement.

4. Multiply the shadow of the tall object (the tree, swing set, etc.) by 12. Then divide that answer by the length of the ruler's shadow. This will give you the height of the swing set (in inches).

Ruler's Shadow = 15 in.
Tree's Shadow = 300 in.

```
  300
x  12
 600
 300
3600
```

```
        240
15 ) 3600
     30
     ---
      60
      60
      ---
       0
```

Tree is 240 in. tall or 20 ft.

Sun-Dried Apples

What to Use

- apples
- knife
- cheese cloth
- old sheet
- plastic bags and ties

What to Do

1. Peel the apples and take the cores out.

2. Slice the apples crossways to form rings.

3. Place an old sheet on a picnic table or other hard surface in the hot sun. Spread the apple slices on the sheet and cover them with cheese cloth to keep the bugs away.

4. Turn the apples when the tops are dry to allow the other side to dry. This should take several days. Take the apples in at night to protect them from moisture.

5. Store the dried apple slices in tightly closed plastic bags or in air-tight tins.

A delicious spicy pie made from these apple slices on a cold winter day will fill the kitchen with memories almost as warm as the summer sun. Peaches, pears, and apricots can be dried this way, too.

chewy gooey fruit leather

Use the sun to help you make a yummy fruit anytime snack.

What to Use

- 2 quarts of very ripe fresh fruit
  (apricots or berries or peaches)
- ¼ C sugar or honey
- collander or sieve
- large cooking pot and spoon
- table knife
- waxed paper and masking tape
- stove
- adult help

What to Do

1. Wash the fruit, take out all stems and seeds and cut any large pieces in half.

2. Put the fruit into the pot and mix in the sugar or honey.
   Cook it over low heat until the fruit is soft.

3. Pour off the juice. Cool the mixture until it can be handled.
   Then press it through the sieve.

4. Lay down a large sheet of waxed paper outside on a table or other flat surface.
   Tape it on the corners so it won't blow away in the wind.

5. Pour the mixture on the waxed paper and let it dry for a couple of days. When the fruit
   leather peels away from the paper easily, it is ready to eat.

6. Cut it in strips and store it in a cool place.

143

Solarberry Jam

You really can use solar energy to make jam if you plan ahead. This strawberry jam should be made a day or two before you want to use it because the flavor improves with time.

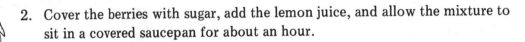

What to Use

- measuring cup
- measuring spoons
- saucepan
- stove, hot plate, or campfire

- 1 cup sugar
- 1 tbsp. lemon juice
- 1 lb. strawberries

What to Do

1. Early in the morning, take the stems off the strawberries and wash them carefully.

2. Cover the berries with sugar, add the lemon juice, and allow the mixture to sit in a covered saucepan for about an hour.

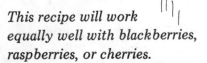

3. Put the saucepan on the heat and bring the mixture to a boil. Boil for about five minutes and then remove from heat.

4. Let the berry mixture sit again for about an hour. Then spoon it into a shallow baking dish and cover it with clear plastic wrap.

5. Put the pan outside in the sunniest spot possible. Leave it all day.

This recipe will work equally well with blackberries, raspberries, or cherries.

6. Pour the mixture into a jelly jar. Store your jam in the refrigerator to save it for your "Solar Celebration" brunch.

Your Own Sundial

A sundial tells you sun time. A special pointer, called a GNOMON, casts a shadow that marks the hours. The shadow moves as the sun moves across the sky. Here's how you can make your own sundial.

What to Use

- round piece of wood or very heavy cardboard
- glob of modeling clay
- long pencil or knitting needle (for the gnomon)
- pen or pencil
- watch or clock
- compass

What to Do

1. Mark the center of the circle and draw a line that divides the circle in half, passing through the center.

2. Put the glob of clay exactly in the center of the circle and stick the eraser end of the pencil or the fat end of the needle in the clay so that it stands up very straight.

3. On a sunny morning, get up early with the sun. Use your compass to find north and point the end of the line north. Set the sundial in a place where it will get sun all day.

4. Use a clock to help you number the dial. Each hour, look at the board to see where the shadow of the gnomon is and make a mark. Write the hour at the end of the mark. DO NOT MOVE THE BOARD. Be sure to do this every hour until the sun sets.

5. On any other sunny day, you can set the dial pointing north and use it as a clock. It will tell you the approximate sun time where you live.

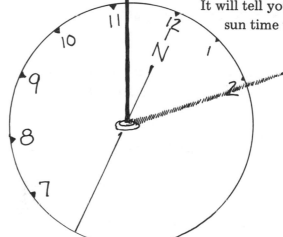

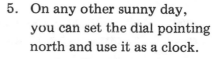

Easy Solar Greenhouse

You can make your own greenhouse that holds the sun's heat to keep your plants warm on cold nights!

What to Do

1. Prepare the ground for planting along the side of a garage, house or shed. Choose a spot that faces south.

2. Lean several thin wood slats up against the wall of the building. Put the slats about three feet apart. Be sure your slats are long enough and far enough apart to leave some room for plants.

3. Cut pieces of heavy plastic large enough to cover the slats from top to bottom and hang over the ends to the ground. (See next page.)

4. Arrange the plastic over the wood, nailing it firmly at the top of each slat and taping sheets together where they overlap. The plastic needs to fit tightly over the whole area so that no cold air can sneak in.

5. Paint several large cans on the top and sides with black paint.

6. When the paint is dry, fill the cans with water, put the tops on, and stack them along the back of the greenhouse area. The black paint will attract the heat of the sun during the day and warm the water inside. This warmth will keep the plants warm at night.

What to Use

- wood for slats
- hammer and nails
- heavy plastic sheeting
- heavy tape (such as duct tape)
- several large cans with tops
- black paint
- paint brush
- hose or other water supply
- several bricks

7. Now you have your little greenhouse and it's time to plant!

8. On warm, sunny days, uncover the greenhouse so the sun can shine on the plants and the solar collectors.

9. On cold days and at night, close up the greenhouse tightly. Put bricks around the bottom edges of the plastic to keep the warmth in and the cold air out.

What to Do When It's Too Hot

There are just some days when it's SOOOOOO hot that you can hardly stand to move.
Here are some things to do to cool yourself off on those slow, hot days.

GET WET again and again . . .

Make yourself a hat to keep off the hot sun.

Play water games with hoses or spray bottles or water balloons.

Drink a LOT of water.

Offer to wash someone's car.

Dress in light-colored, loose-fitting clothing.

to Do ANYTHING!

Stay in the shade.

Make yourself a fan from paper and a stick.

Mix up some cool drinks. ICE your glass first by putting it in the freezer for ½ hour after you've dipped it in water.

Eat watermelon.

Make yourself some popsicles.

Lie VERY, VERY still.

cool, cool treats for hot, hot days

COOL-YOU-OFF DRINKS

FRUIT FLOATS

Freeze slices of oranges
or cherries
or grapes
or peach slices
or lemon slices

Float them on top of a
tall glass of fruit juice.

FRUIT SODAS

Mix ¼ C mashed fruit
with 1 C soda water and
1 T honey.

Top with 1 scoop of
ice cream.

PEANUTTY SHAKE

Blend 3 T peanut butter
with 2 scoops of vanilla ice
cream and 1 C of milk.

VERY BERRY

Mix strawberries
or raspberries
or blueberries
with 1 C water
or gingerale and
1 T honey.

Blend in blender.

BANANA WHIZ

Whip in blender:
1 mashed banana
2 C milk
½ C orange juice
dash of cinnamon

LEMONGRAPEADE

Stir together grape juice
and lemonade.
Add slices of lemon
and sprigs of mint.

PURPLE COW FIZZ

Add a scoop of ice cream
to: 1 C of grape juice
and 1 C of gingerale.

WHIPPED FLIP

Shake together (or whip in
blender)

1 C orange juice
1 C yogurt or cream
1 T vanilla

YUMSICLES!

What to Use

- popsicle recipes
- small paper cups
- plastic spoons
  or
  popsicle sticks

What to Do

1. Mix any of these mixtures or some you invent.

2. Pour them into small paper cups (or ice cube trays).

3. Freeze until slushy.

4. Put in plastic spoons, or popsicle sticks for handles.

5. Freeze until firm.

6. Peel away the paper cup.

JUICE BARS

Blend 1 C water with 1 C of any kind of concentrated juice.

PURPLE APPLESICLES

Mix 2 Cups of applesauce with 1 Cup of grape juice.

TOOTI-FRUITI-SICLES

Mix 2 Cups of any kind of fruit (no seeds, please) with 1 Cup of fruit juice in a blender.

OJ YOCICLE!

Mix 1 Cup yogurt
1 small can of frozen orange juice
1 teaspoon of vanilla.

SPICY SICLES

Mix 1 Cup of yogurt with 1 teaspoon of nutmeg, 1 teaspoon of cinnamon and 1 Tablespoon of honey.

PUDDING SICLES

Thin your favorite pudding with a little milk. Then freeze it!

BANANA CREMEPOPS

Mix mashed bananas with cream or half and half.

ANYTHING SICLES

Freeze any kind of fruit juice you want!

151

FROZEN FRUIT DELIGHTS

FROZEN BANANAS

-Put a stick in each peeled banana.
-Wrap bananas in foil.
-Freeze 1 hour.
-Dip bananas in melted chocolate chips.
-Dip again in chopped nuts.
-Wrap and freeze another hour or longer.

FRUIT TIDBITS

-Wash and freeze any of these:
    sweet cherries
    melon balls
    peach slices
    grapes

-Then, pop them into your mouth
 frozen . . .
    and enjoy the cool,
    icy taste.

MELON MUSH

-Put watermelon cubes (no seeds)
    a few ice cubes
    a cup of lemonade
in blender and whiz a few seconds.

ORANGE CRUSH

Blend frozen orange juice
    ice cubes
    a cup of gingerale
in a blender at high speed.

TROPICAL SLUSH

Whiz pineapple chunks,
pineapple juice, banana chunks
and a bit of shredded coconut
at high speed in a blender.

SNO-CONES

-Crush ice in a blender. (Whir ice cubes
WITH WATER until ice is crushed. Then
pour off the water.) OR put ice cubes in
an old pillowcase and pound with a
hammer to crush them finely. Then
-Fill a cup ½ full of crushed ice. Pour
over a few tablespoons of any kind
of juice and stir.

Cloudwatching

Cloud watching is relaxing and fascinating. Spend an hour on your back—and you'll be surprised how much goes on up there!

What to Do

1. When you've found a quiet place, lie very still on your back. Look all over the sky to see as many clouds as you can. Let your eyes rest on each cloud.

   What do the clouds look like? *Are they high?* *thick?* *fluffy?* *stringy?* *white?*
   low? *thin?* *bumpy?* *billowy?* *black or grey?*

   Do you see any that have definite characteristics? *noses?* *eyes?* *ears?* *snouts?* *arms?* *antlers?*

   Do you see any that look like animals? *people?* *strange creatures?*

2. Choose a few clouds and name them after people, objects, states, animals. Or give them imaginary names.

3. Watch one particular cloud for several minutes.

   How does it change? *How fast is it moving?*

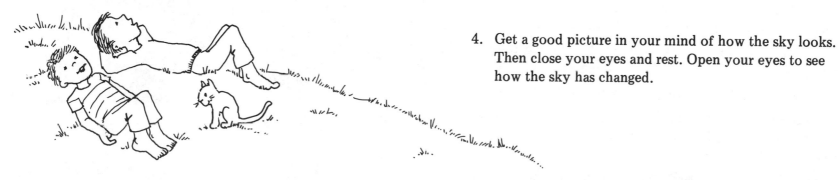

4. Get a good picture in your mind of how the sky looks. Then close your eyes and rest. Open your eyes to see how the sky has changed.

GAMES

KICK THE CAN

for after the sun sets

What to Do

1. The CAN will serve as home base. Choose a spot to put the can. It needs to be in an open area.

2. Decide on the boundaries for your hiding game.

3. Wait until the sun sets, then gather everyone together and explain the rules of the game.

4. Choose someone to be IT and you're ready to begin.

What to Use

– a large tin can
– several players
– an area for the "jail"

RULES OF THE GAME:

* IT stays at the can, covers her eyes, and counts to 50 while the other players hide.

* Then IT tries to find the others. When she sees someone, she must run and touch the can and say "I see _____."

* A player is safe if he can run and kick the can before IT gets to the can and says his name.

* When IT catches a hider, that person must stay in the "jail" area.

* If there is only one person left hiding, and she gets to the can and kicks it before IT catches her, then ALL the players in the jail are freed! Then IT is IT for another game.

* Choose another IT (perhaps the first person caught) for the next round.

iles from us,

the night sky.

What to Use

- clear night
- notebook and pencil
- book on stars (from your library)
- small flashlight
- telescope or binoculars if available

o look for! There are some suggestions on
pages. It is also a good idea to get a map of
looks in each season. Star maps can be found
books.

to start gazing!

What to Use

small jars with tops
bag of unpopped popcorn
20 people wearing DARK
thes

haking his also.

Stargazing

There are billions of stars that shine in the sky. Even though they're millions of [?]
we folks here on earth can see plenty of them.

You'll learn a lot, and have a good time too, if you get in the habit of examining [?]
Do it all year round because the sky changes as the earth moves around the sun.

What to Do

1. Read the Stargazer's Rules (on the next page) before you set out to gaze into the night.

2. The first time you go out, just spend some time looking and enjoying the whole display of stars before you look for specific ones.

3. Get a book from the library on astronomy. It will give you fascinating information and teach you how and where and when to locate stars, planets, constellations, and other heavenly bodies.

4. Know what the next tw[?] how the sky in many sta[?]

5. You're read[?]

STARGAZER'S RULES

* Choose a clear, dark night.

* Find a place that is as dark as possible, away from house lights or street lights.

* Give your eyes time to adjust to the dark.

* Lie on your back if possible and hold very still.

* Fix your eyes on one star at a time and watch it for awhile.

* Keep your star maps or star books handy to check locations of stars. Use your flashlight to help you see the book. Make notes or drawings in your notebook. Always write the date you saw a star or other things in the sky.

* Watch lights carefully. If a light moves steadily, it may be a satellite or plane instead of a star.

WHAT TO WATCH FOR

STARS *Stars move very slowly. They seem to twinkle. Stars have their own names. Try to learn the names and locations of some of the brightest stars:*

Sirius	*Capella*
Antares	*Betelgeuse*
Spica	*Altair*

THE NORTH STAR *Polaris, the North Star, is a very special star because it seems to move hardly at all. It is always north. When you're looking at Polaris, you're looking north. It can help you find your way when you're lost. To find it, use a compass and look to the north. Or, find the Little Dipper. It is the last star in the handle of the Little Dipper.*

PLANETS *You might be able to see VENUS just after sunset. It is very bright. MARS is a steady, reddish light. JUPITER is steady and more white than stars. SATURN is a yellow light.*

METEORS *These are called shooting stars. They make streaks in the sky and are usually seen after midnight.*

CONSTELLATIONS *Constellations are groups of stars that seem to form a picture in the sky. Watch for those that are shown on the next page and others you find in your star book.*

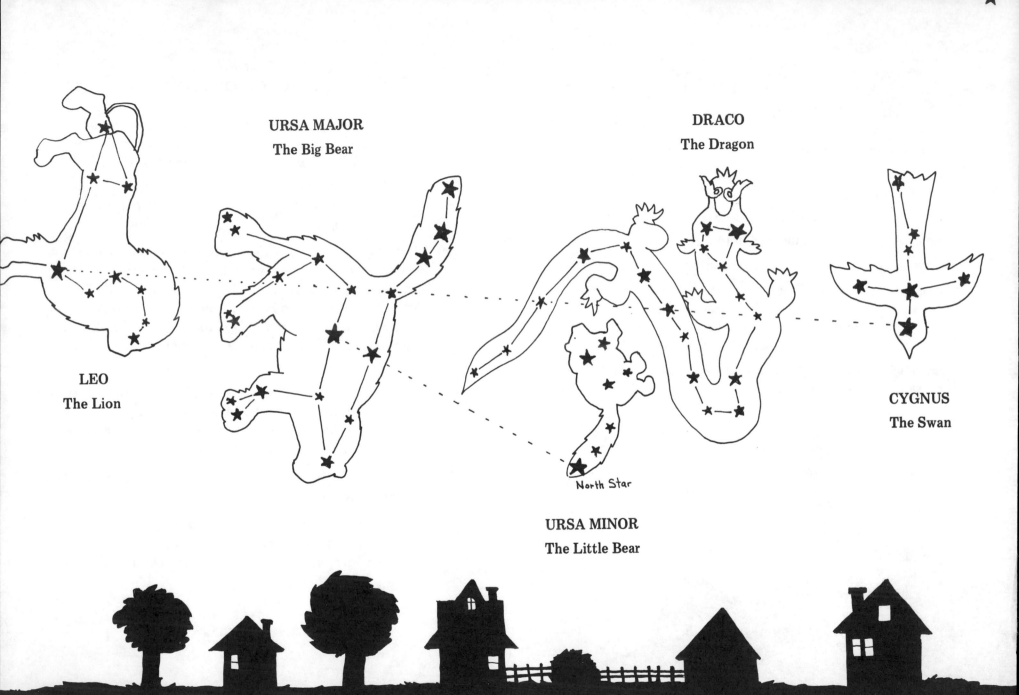

URSA MAJOR

The Big Bear

DRACO

The Dragon

LEO

The Lion

CYGNUS

The Swan

North Star

URSA MINOR

The Little Bear

Moonwatch

As the moon orbits the earth, its appearance changes to those of us who are watching it from earth. The orbit takes about 29½ days. During the first part of this time, the moon is WAXING (increasing in size) and later, the moon is WANING (decreasing in size). Keep your own moonwatch for a month to see how the moon changes!!

What to Do

1. Find out from a calendar or a weather station when the next new moon will be.

2. Make a calendar that begins with that day and continues for 30 days. On your calendar, leave space to write.

3. Try to watch for the moon every day for 30 days. Each evening, write on your calendar what time the moon rises and draw a picture showing how it looks.

   Watch the changes carefully!

   How many days does the WAXING take?

   How many days is the moon FULL?

   How many days does the WANING take?

   Does the moon ever rise during the day?

What to Use

- large piece of drawing paper
- ruler
- crayons
- pencil

☽ Jan 9 4:01 p.m.	☽ 10 4:45 p.m.	☽ 11 5:25 p.m.	☽ 12 6:20 p.m.	☽ 13 7:02 p.m.	☽ 14 7:50 p.m.	☽ 15 8:30 p.m.
☽ 16 9:11 p.m.	☽ 17 10:00 p.m.	◒ 18 too late	◒ 19	○ 20	○ 21	22
23	24	25	26	27	28	29
30	31	Feb 1	2	3	4	5
6	7					

A Moonlight Hike

At least once a season, gather your family together on a moonlit night and go for a hike.
You'll be surprised at how different the world looks by moonlight!

What to Do

1. LISTEN! *What do you hear that you wouldn't hear during the daytime?*
Do you hear animal sounds?   Count the different ones.
Can you hear water?   Grasses?   Trees?
Listen to the sounds of your feet in the snow or leaves or grass or dirt.
Who else is out tonight?   What sounds do they make?

2. WATCH! *How does the sky look at night?   How are the clouds different from daytime clouds?*
Can you see the moon rise and move across the sky?   What is its size and shape?
How do trees and bushes look against a dark sky?   How do flowers look at night?
How do colors change?
What strange shapes are taken on by houses?   Cars?   People?

Hurrah For Things That Creep & Crawl & Swim & Fly!

BUGGED!

Are you bugged by all those little creatures that buzz and bite and crawl around your house and yard? Take a close look at the little animals who bug you. They really are an interesting bunch. Once you get to know them, you'll probably like them better!

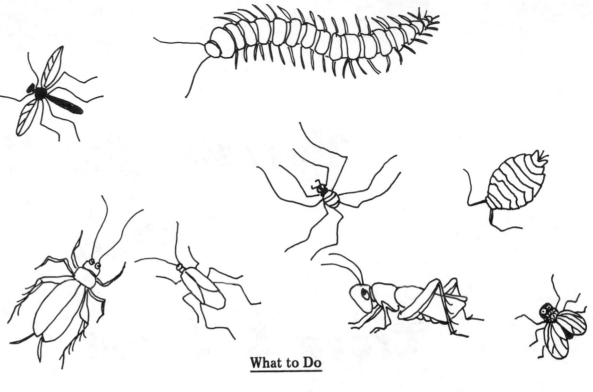

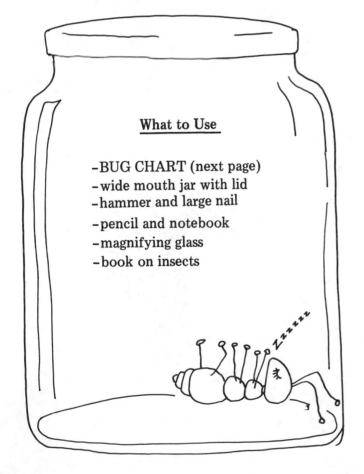

What to Use

- BUG CHART (next page)
- wide mouth jar with lid
- hammer and large nail
- pencil and notebook
- magnifying glass
- book on insects

What to Do

1. Take some time to go bugwatching. One very good place to do this is around your porch light at night. Light attracts many bugs so you have a ready-made collection.

2. Use the BUG CHART or your insect book to try to identify the bugs you find. Make notes in your notebook about what you've seen.

3. If you want to take a closer, longer look at any bugs, catch them in a wide mouth jar. Make sure you've poked holes in the lid so they can have air. Or make yourself an Insect Observatory (found later in this chapter). Keep the bugs in the jar until you're done examining them, then set them free.

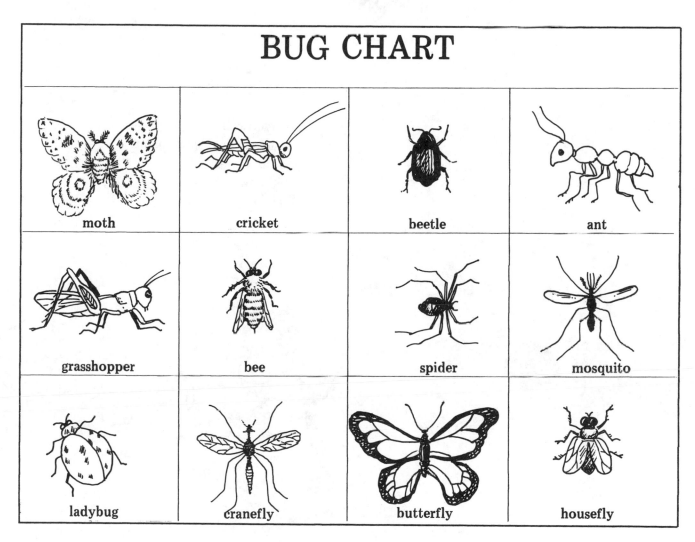

BUG CHART

moth	cricket	beetle	ant
grasshopper	bee	spider	mosquito
ladybug	cranefly	butterfly	housefly

There are many different varieties of bees, flies, butterflies, moths, beetles and spiders.
So you may see some that look a bit different from the pictures here.

Web Snatching

What to Use

-spider web
-black enamel spray paint
-white paper
-old newspapers
-scissors

Try snatching a spider web some day when the spider isn't home! Don't worry, the spider will quickly build a new web!

What to Do

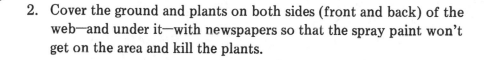

1. Look for a good spider web on your next nature walk.

2. Cover the ground and plants on both sides (front and back) of the web—and under it—with newspapers so that the spray paint won't get on the area and kill the plants.

3. Stand about three feet away from the front of the web, and spray it lightly with the paint. Then do the same from the back of the web. Don't spray too much, or the web will start to sag.

4. Bend your paper and bring the center of it to the center of the web. Since the web will still be wet, it will stick to the paper easily. Pull the web very carefully away from its moorings—if necessary, cut the lines that hold it in place.

5. Allow the web to dry thoroughly. Then cut your paper down to just a little larger than the web, and mount the entire work on black paper.

Make Friends with a Worm

What to Use

- worms
- old aquarium or other glass container
- food for the worms
- black paper and tape
- soil, sand, dead leaves
- magnifying glass
- drawing paper and pencil
- shovel
- water

What to Do

1. CATCH SOME EARTHWORMS: Dig for them in the soil in your yard at night when they're close to the surface. Or pick up some worms that have come out of the ground during a heavy rainfall.

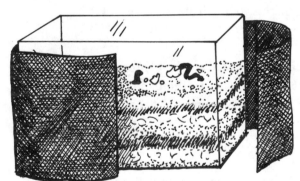

2. BUILD THEM A HOME: Put layers of soil, dead leaves and sand in an old aquarium or other large, deep glass container. Sprinkle water on each layer. Cover the outside of the glass with dark paper so that the worms will tunnel close to the glass. Keep this paper on except for times when you're observing the worms. Add a shovel full of worms. Keep the container covered but punch some small air holes in the lid.

3. CARE FOR THE WORMS: Feed them pieces of lettuce, dead leaves, grass clippings or bits of table food. Lay bits of food on the surface of their home. (Remove uneaten food so it doesn't spoil.) Be sure to keep the soil moist by sprinkling on a little water every day.

4. OBSERVE THE WORMS: * Watch the worms move and tunnel around in the dirt.

   * Look for CASTINGS in the dirt. As the earthworm eats its way through the firmer soil, the soil passes through its body and out onto the ground forming CASTINGS that look like little piles of fine dirt.

   * Take a worm out of its home. Use a magnifying glass to find the SETAE on the underside of the worm. (These are the worm's "feet.")

   * Watch how the worm moves by squeezing and contracting its muscles. Draw a picture of how the earthworm looks as it moves.

   * Find the worm's head. Does it have eyes? Does it have ears?

   * Look behind the first segment to find its mouth. Use a magnifying glass if you need to.

   * Count the worm's segments. You can tell a worm's age by the number of segments. Adult worms have about 110. Young worms have fewer.

   * Measure different worms in your collection.

   * Spread out all the worms once in a while to see the cocoons.

5. EXPERIMENT:

   * Worms can feel some vibrations. Try playing music near the worms to see if they come to the surface. Outside, try tapping on the ground.

Ants,

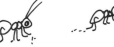 

*Build an ant colony so you can observe the
wonderful ways of the ants.*

What to Use

- loose soil and ants
- small shovel or large spoon
- magnifying glass
- food for the ants
- large jar with lid
- small narrow jar with lid (This jar should be a little shorter
  than the large jar and should be narrow enough to fit inside
  the large jar with space around it for dirt.)
- nail and hammer
- black paper and masking tape
- small sponge
- water

What to Do

1. Put the top on the small jar and set it inside
   the large jar.

2. Poke very tiny holes in the lid of the large jar.
   These holes need to be smaller than an ant.

Ants,

3. Dig up some ants. Look for a place where the soil is loose or
   find an ant hill. Use a small shovel to take up some ants and
   soil together. You must have a queen in your ant colony.
   The queen ant is larger than the other ants.

4. Put the dirt and ants into the space between the narrow jar
   and the large jar.

5. Cover the jar with black paper so the ants will tunnel close to the glass. Tape the paper in place. Keep the paper on except for observation times.

6. Take good care of the ants: feed them tiny crumbs of bread, bird seed, smashed up dog food, or other small food bits. Keep a damp (not soaking wet) sponge lying on top of the small jar inside the ants' home AT ALL TIMES.

7. Observe the ants often:
   * *What do they spend their time doing?*
   * *Watch them carry food. How do they handle large pieces?*
   * *Do they communicate with each other? How?*

8. Take out a few ants for closer watching. Use a magnifying glass.
   * *How do they get around an obstacle in their path?*
   * *Can you find an ant's eyes? mouth? antennae?*
   * *Find out how fast an ant travels.*

  **Everywhere!**

insect observatory

One of the best ways to learn about a particular insect is to observe it carefully for a day or two. You can do this in your home-made creature catcher!

What to Use

-some wire screening
-scissors
-two jar lids (the same size)
-thin wire
-adult help

What to Do

1. Cut the screen the height you want your observatory to be. It should be wide enough to fit inside the jar lids and overlap a little bit.

2. Roll the screen into a tube shape.

3. Put a jar lid on either side of the tube.

4. Tie a strand of wire around the screen to hold the sides together.

5. Put soil and twigs or a plant inside to make the observatory as nearly like the insect's home as possible. You will want to be sure that there is plenty of light, food, and air.

6. Catch an insect and put it into the observatory by removing one lid. Return your displaced insect back to its natural habitat just as soon as you have learned all you need to know about it.

Creeper Crawler Creature Log

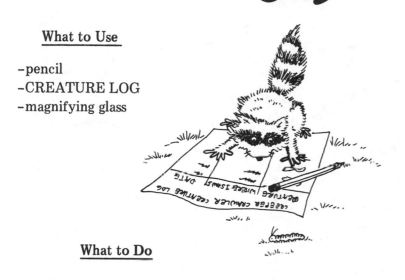

What to Use

-pencil
-CREATURE LOG
-magnifying glass

What to Do

1. Watch for creatures around your neighborhood. Keep your CREATURE LOG handy and have a magnifying glass with you for close-up views.

2. When you find a creeper or crawler, write down the date and the place you saw it.

3. See if you can find each creature on the list.

4. Add others to the list if you see some that aren't pictured here. Draw a picture of each new creature.

CREATURE LOG		
Creature	Where I Saw It	Dates
Caterpillar		
Centipede		
Millipede		
Earthworm		
Snail		
Frog		
Spider		
Mouse		
Rabbit		
Others:		
Others:		

The Fish That DIDN'T Get Away

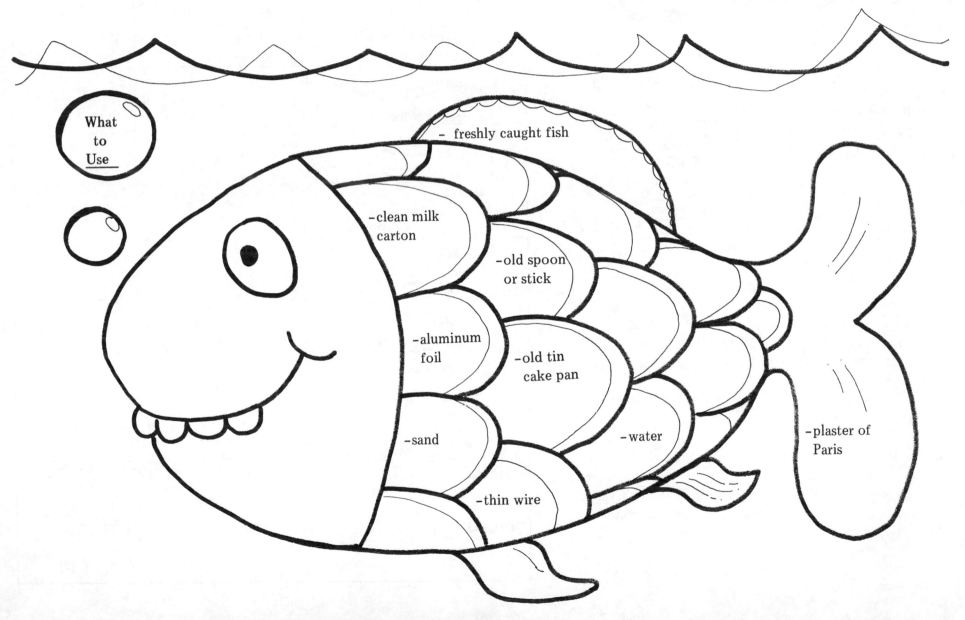

What to Use

- freshly caught fish
- clean milk carton
- old spoon or stick
- aluminum foil
- old tin cake pan
- sand
- water
- thin wire
- plaster of Paris

What to Do

1. Line the pan with aluminum foil.

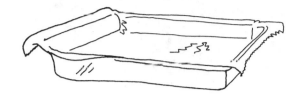

2. Fill the pan with sand.

3. Dampen the sand with water and smooth it out.

4. Push the fish into the sand.

5. Mix the plaster of Paris and water to form a soft paste. Follow the package directions for best results.

6. Firmly push the fish into the sand again and then take it out.

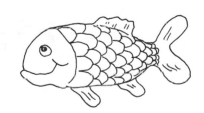

7. Quickly fill the impression left by the fish with plaster of Paris.

8. Bend the thin wire into a loop and push it into the plaster of Paris to form a hanger.

9. Set the pan aside in a dry place for about two days.

10. Remove your fish plaque and hang it on the wall!

do-it-yourself Backyard Pond

What to Use

-child's swimming pool
-small fish
-tadpoles
-plants
-pond water (if possible)

What to Do

1. Fill the pool with water. Some water that you bring from a pond is the best.

2. Put some plants into your pond. You can get plants from a store that sells fish or you might transplant a few from a pond area. (Get permission to do this.)

3. Put some animals in your pond. Start with animals that you catch in a pond or puddles. Try catching some toads or tadpoles or crayfish. You can also add small fish from a pet store.

4. Wait and watch your pond over a period of several days and weeks. Other animals will be attracted to the pond.

Quick-and-Easy Birdhouse

What to Do

1. Cut two round holes across from each other in the biggest part of the bleach bottle.

2. Glue the pie tin to the bottom of the bottle to make a ledge.

3. Tie the cord around the neck of the bottle to make a hanging loop.

4. Put a little birdseed in the bottom of the bottle and hang the nest from a tree branch.

What to Use

- large plastic bleach bottle, thoroughly cleaned
- sturdy scissors
- glue
- aluminum pie tin
- strong cord
- birdseed

175

Strictly for the Birds

. . . A TASTY GARLAND

What to Use

- heavy sewing thread
- large needle
- brightly colored yarn or ribbon
- chunks of uncooked animal fat
- pieces of apple or pear

What to Do

1. Thread the needle with a good, long length of thread.

2. String small chunks of fat and pieces of fruit on the thread. (Don't put on too many or your garland will be too heavy to hang.)

3. Push the chunks of fat and the pieces of fruit apart leaving enough room to tie ribbon or yarn bows between each piece. The bright colors will help to attract the birds' attention.

4. Loop the garland over a tree branch or shrub to give the birds a special treat on a cold winter day.

. . . A WINTERTIME DINNER

Many years ago, people in Scandinavia would hang a sheaf of grain in their gardens to feed the birds during the cold, hard winter. As this custom spread through northern Europe, it became a symbol of hope for a fruitful year to come. It was believed that if many birds came to feast on the grain sheaf, the garden would do well during the next growing season.

Even if you don't have a garden, you can still carry out the custom.

What to Do

1. Tie wheat, oats or barley together with some pine cones and hang the sheaf to a tree branch.

2. Tie several small branches of grain to a shrub that is easily accessible to small birds.

3. Use a wire hanger to make a hanging loop for an ear of dried corn. Be sure to push the ends of the wire into the corn ear so the birds won't hurt themselves while feasting.

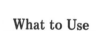

What to Use

- pine cones
- pieces of various grains
- dried ear of corn
- wire hanger

177

. . . A PEANUT BUTTER SANDWICH!

What to Use

- a stale donut
- sturdy string
- nail
- hammer
- two jar lids of the same size
- peanut butter
- table knife

What to Do

1. Use the hammer to drive the nail through the center of one jar lid.

2. Center the donut hole on the nail.

Dear Wild Songbirds,
Please come to a dinner party in your home.
Time: any time
Place: in my back yard

With love, Angie

3. Use the hammer to drive the end of the nail through the other jar lid. This makes a sandwich—one jar lid, the donut, the other jar lid.

4. Spread the sides of the donut with peanut butter.

5. Tie the string securely around the nail to make a hanging loop.

6. Hang the donut sandwich from a tree branch or from your window sill.

Spiffy

PEANUT BUTTER

. . . A PICNIC IN A PINE CONE

What to Use

- a large pine cone
- thick twine
- spoon and bowl
- ½ cup salad oil
- 1 cup peanut butter
- about 2 cups birdseed
- paper bag
- small knife

What to Do

1. If you find more pine cones than you need, bring some extra ones for friends and ask them to help you feed the birds.

2. Twist the twine around the pine cone and tie it securely to make a hanging loop.

3. Use the spoon to mix the peanut butter and salad oil together in the bowl. Then spread the mixture between the petals of the pine cone.

4. Put the pine cone and birdseed in the paper bag and shake it gently up and down to coat the peanut butter-covered cone with seeds.

5. Hang the pine cone on a tree or window sill where you can watch the birds as they picnic.

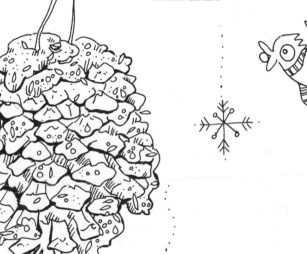

Donations to a Bird's Nest

Everyone needs a home, including the birds that fly around your neighborhood. Here is a way to help them find materials for building their nests. This ought to make you famous in bird circles!

What to Use

- strips of string, fabric and yarn
- wire hanger
- piece of wide mesh material such as an orange or potato bag from the grocery store

What to Do

1. Bend your wire hanger into a square or rectangular shape.

2. Attach the mesh material to it. If you use a potato sack, simply drape the bag over the hanger. If you use some other material, tie it on with string or glue it into place.

3. Loosely weave yarn, fabric strips, and string through the mesh.

4. In early spring, hang your nest-building helper in a tree near your window. Watch as the neighborhood birds flock to it to choose the materials they need.

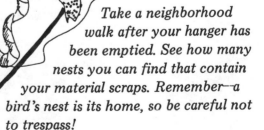

Take a neighborhood walk after your hanger has been emptied. See how many nests you can find that contain your material scraps. Remember—a bird's nest is its home, so be careful not to trespass!

180

Airplane Acrobatics

What to Use

- 8½ x 11 inch typing paper
- ruler
- scissors

What to Do

1. Fold the paper in half, crease it and then open it up.

2. Fold the long edge of the paper in ¼ inch. Repeat this 10 times or until the paper is about 4½ inches long.

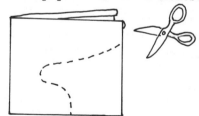

3. Fold the paper in half again and cut a line like this one shown.

Hold a paper airplane contest with all the kids in your neighborhood. Each of you can design your own plane!

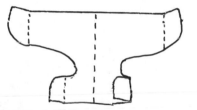

4. Open up the plane and fold the wing tips in toward the center.

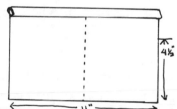

5. Turn the plane over and fold the tips of the tail wings in toward the center.

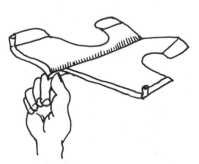

6. Hold the airplane with the fold in your fingertips and take it out for a test flight. Throw it gently from a high place such as a window or a chair.

What to Use

-two sticks of lightweight, flexible wood
 (one a little shorter than the other)
-tissue paper or lightweight plastic
-lots of kite string
-liquid white glue or rubber cement
-small, sharp knife
-scissors
-paint, crayons or markers for kite decorations

My Favorite Kite

What to Do

1. Use the knife to make a notch about 1½ inches deep into both ends of each stick.

2. Lay the shorter stick across the longer one about a third of the way down on the long stick. Use a piece of string to tie the two sticks together securely.

3. Starting at the bottom, run one piece of string all the way around the outside of the kite. Put it through the notches in each of the sticks. Keep the string tight as you work. Tie strong knots at the places where you begin and end. Leave a long tail of string hanging from the bottom.

182

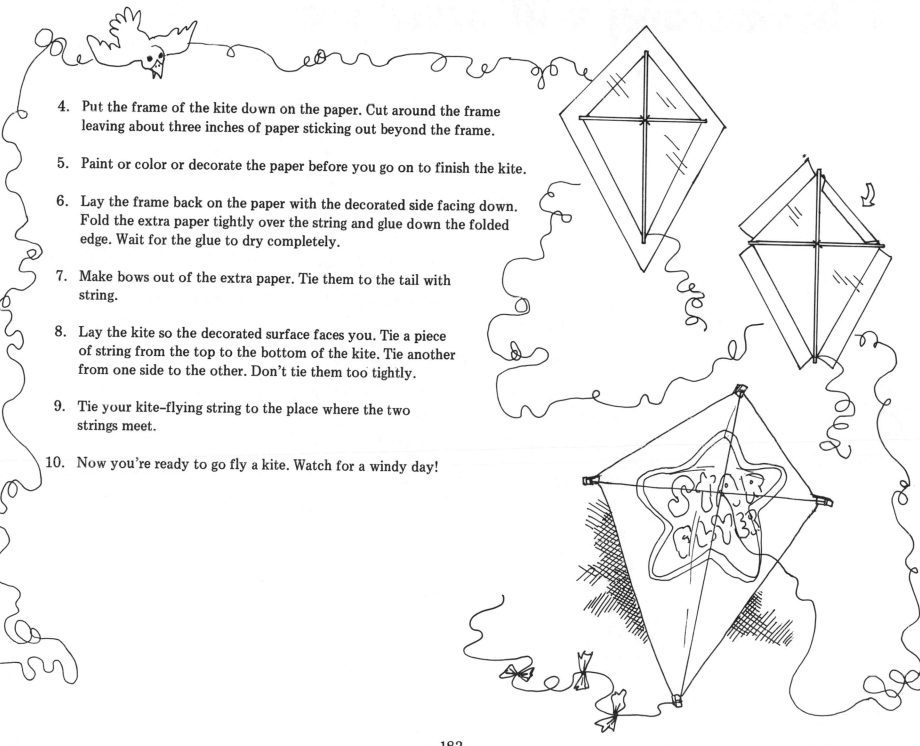

4. Put the frame of the kite down on the paper. Cut around the frame leaving about three inches of paper sticking out beyond the frame.

5. Paint or color or decorate the paper before you go on to finish the kite.

6. Lay the frame back on the paper with the decorated side facing down. Fold the extra paper tightly over the string and glue down the folded edge. Wait for the glue to dry completely.

7. Make bows out of the extra paper. Tie them to the tail with string.

8. Lay the kite so the decorated surface faces you. Tie a piece of string from the top to the bottom of the kite. Tie another from one side to the other. Don't tie them too tightly.

9. Tie your kite-flying string to the place where the two strings meet.

10. Now you're ready to go fly a kite. Watch for a windy day!

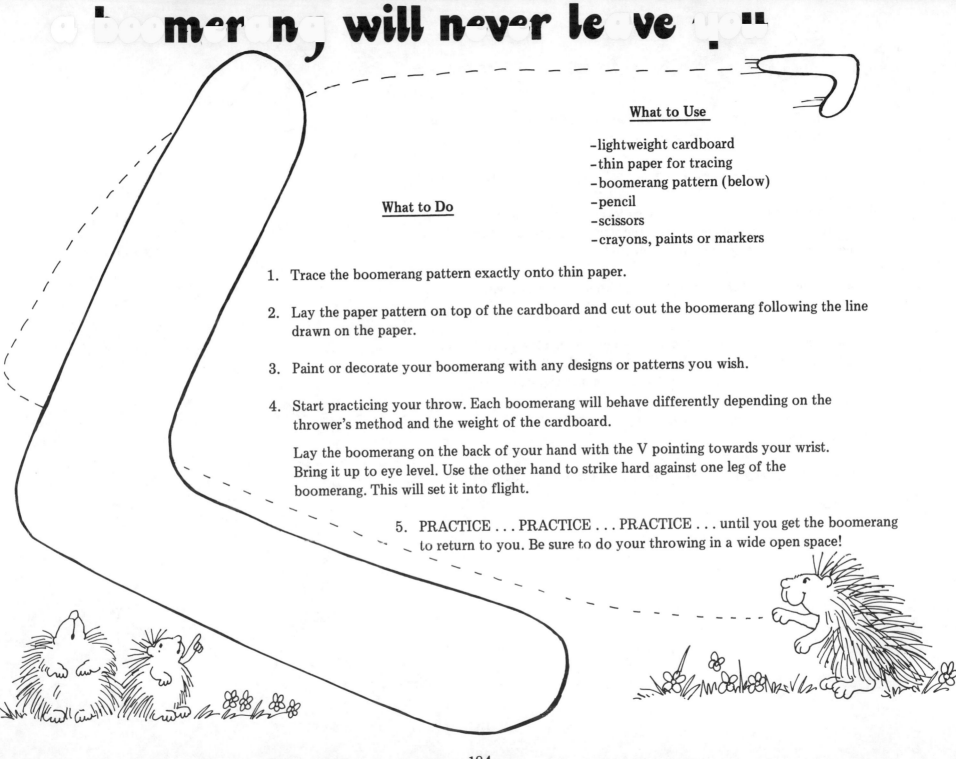

"a boomerang will never leave you"

What to Use

- lightweight cardboard
- thin paper for tracing
- boomerang pattern (below)
- pencil
- scissors
- crayons, paints or markers

What to Do

1. Trace the boomerang pattern exactly onto thin paper.

2. Lay the paper pattern on top of the cardboard and cut out the boomerang following the line drawn on the paper.

3. Paint or decorate your boomerang with any designs or patterns you wish.

4. Start practicing your throw. Each boomerang will behave differently depending on the thrower's method and the weight of the cardboard.

   Lay the boomerang on the back of your hand with the V pointing towards your wrist. Bring it up to eye level. Use the other hand to strike hard against one leg of the boomerang. This will set it into flight.

5. PRACTICE . . . PRACTICE . . . PRACTICE . . . until you get the boomerang to return to you. Be sure to do your throwing in a wide open space!

Hurrah For Seasons!

Snow Stuff

Need some things to do on a snowy day??
Try some of these!

TRASH BAG SLIDE

Find a gentle slope that's covered with snow. A slanting driveway will work, too. Sit on the garbage bag. Ask a friend to give you a push!

SNOW SCULPTURES

Do this on a day when the snow is slightly wet, so that it will pack well. Try sculpting snow persons and snow animals and snow vehicles and . . . . . .

SNOW ANGELS
and other creatures.

Lie in the snow. Move your arms and legs to make angels or other creations. Can you make an elephant? a cat? an anteater? a flamingo?

186

SNOW FORTS

Use your hands, small shovels or large spoons
to dig big holes and tunnels into snowbanks.
Carved out snowbanks made wonderful
forts!

FOX & GEESE

In your yard or in an open field, make
a winding path with circles and loops.
The path must end back where it
began, to form a huge loop. Make
some flat "base" areas. Then, one person
should be the fox. The rest are the
geese. The fox chases the geese (on the
path only) and tries to catch one. When a
goose is caught, she/he becomes the fox.
The "bases" are rest areas for the geese.
A fox may NOT catch a goose on a base.

SNOW CONES

Put some soft, clean snow in a paper cup. Sprinkle a few
spoons full of powdered juice mix or lemonade over the
top. Mix the snow until all of it is flavored. Enjoy eating
your snow cone with your tongue or with your spoon.

187

Groundhog Shadows

GROUNDHOG DAY is February 2. The legend says that the groundhog comes out of his hole on this day and looks around. If it is a cloudy day and he can't see his shadow, he stays out and winter comes to an end. But, if it is sunny enough for a shadow, the groundhog is frightened by his shadow and returns to his hole—making winter stay around for another six weeks.

On February 2, watch the weather carefully. If it is sunny, try to catch your shadow on paper (or draw it in snow with a stick or on a sidewalk with chalk). If you can catch your shadow, that probably means that the groundhog has seen his, and winter will stay around!

What to Use

- large mural paper
- a friend
- dark crayons
- scissors

What to Do

1. Take a large piece of mural paper. Lay it near you where it will catch your shadow. Stand very still so a friend can trace your shadow with a crayon.

2. Try tracing the shadows of your dog or cat or a groundhog, if you can find one!

3. Cut out the shadows and look at them carefully. Are they scary enough to frighten a groundhog??

   YOU PREDICT! Will the groundhog stay out of his hole today?? Will you have a long winter?

4. Six weeks from today, see if your prediction was right!

Four Leaf Clover Lucky Charm

It's not every day that you'll find a four-leaf clover. But just in case you do, here's a way to preserve it and maybe stretch the good luck it brings.

What to Use

- four-leaf clover
- clean white paper
- heavy book
- clear contact paper
- light blue or gray construction paper
- scissors (pinking shears if possible)
- iron
- adult help

What to Do

1. Put the four-leaf clover between two sheets of clean white paper and leave it in the book to dry for several days. (If you put some weight on top of the book, it will help to press the clover.)

2. Cut a small square of construction paper, then cut a strip of contact paper long enough to fold over and make a case for the square.

3. Take your four-leaf clover from the book and arrange it in the middle of the paper square.

4. Enclose the square in the contact paper strip. Trim to fit and press the edges with a warm iron to seal.

5. Carry your lucky charm with you wherever you go— or, give it to a good friend on St. Patrick's Day.

If you can't find a four-leaf clover, you can glue an extra leaf onto a three-leaf clover.

Special Valentines

Stuff three fat little sachet pillows with dried rose petals, sachet, and good wishes!

OR

Make a potpourri string for a Valentine closet.

1

What to Use

- scissors
- fabric (dotted swiss, silk, satin, or velvet)
- needle and thread
- ribbon and/or lace
- dried rose petals
- dry sachet or perfume

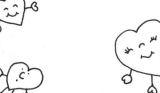

2

What to Use

- red and/or pink net
- scissors
- dried flower petals, orange peels, and cinnamon
- yarn
- spoon

What to Do

1. Cut two hearts for each sachet pillow.

2. Stitch the hearts together leaving an opening at the top.

3. Fill the pillow with dried rose petals and add the sachet or perfume.

4. Push the mixture around with your fingers to get rid of the bumps.

5. Stitch up the opening.

6. Add the ribbon and/or lace for trim.

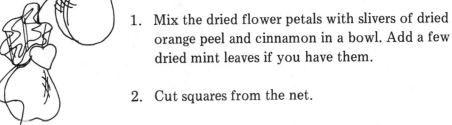
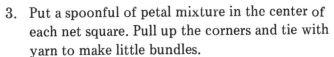
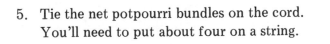

What to Do

1. Mix the dried flower petals with slivers of dried orange peel and cinnamon in a bowl. Add a few dried mint leaves if you have them.

2. Cut squares from the net.

3. Put a spoonful of petal mixture in the center of each net square. Pull up the corners and tie with yarn to make little bundles.

4. Braid or twist a long strand of yarn.

5. Tie the net potpourri bundles on the cord. You'll need to put about four on a string.

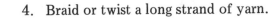
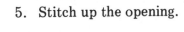

OR   *Arrange a Blooming Hearts centerpiece.*

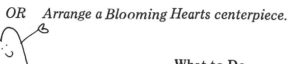

What to Do

3

1. Fill the pot (or can) with fluffy shrubbery branches.

2. Cut out several sizes of paper hearts in pairs.

3. Pair up the hearts and glue each set to the end of a branch (one heart on each side of the branch). Glue enough on to make your pot of branches bloom with paper hearts.

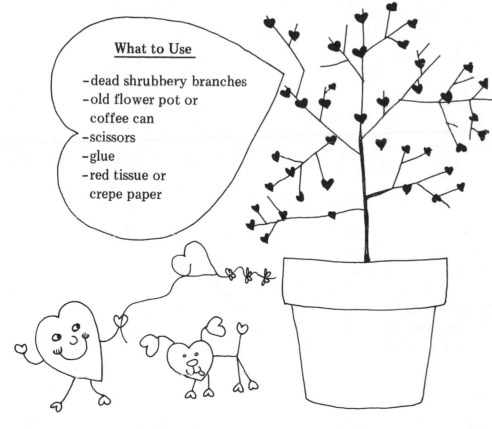

What to Use

- dead shrubbery branches
- old flower pot or coffee can
- scissors
- glue
- red tissue or crepe paper

OR   *Whip up a lacy nosegay!*

What to Do

1. Poke the dried flowers, herbs, and/or weeds through the center of the lace paper doily and pull it up around the back to form a sort of frame. Fill in with sprigs of greenery or small blossoms from house plants if you have them.

4

2. Make a tissue paper cone for the stems and tie them with a pretty bow.

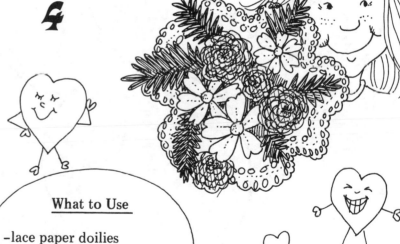

What to Use

- lace paper doilies
- pink and purple tissue paper
- ribbon
- dried wheat, sea oats, baby's breath, mint, sage, honeysuckle (whatever grows in your part of the country)

Rites of Spring Piñata

What to Use

- large balloon
- newspaper
- scissors
- liquid starch or thin
  flour-and-water paste
- shallow pie pan or bowl
- glue
- masking tape
- leaves
- wild flowers, twigs, tree buds,
  bits of bark, leaves
- string

What to Do

1. Cut several strips of newspaper into thin strips.

2. Blow up the balloon and tie it securely.

3. Cover the entire balloon with newspaper strips dipped in starch or paste.

For years, Mexican children have enjoyed the fruits, nuts and candies that fall from broken piñatas during the Christmas season. There's no reason this lovely custom has to be reserved for the Christmas season, however. This "Rites of Spring" Piñata is just one idea. Maybe you can design a special Valentine or birthday piñata, or a Halloween or Thanksgiving one.

4. Apply enough smooth layers of the strips to make a solid covering on the balloon. Let this dry for a few days.

5. Carefully cut a small opening in the base of the dry piñata and push wrapped candies and/or small favors into the opening.

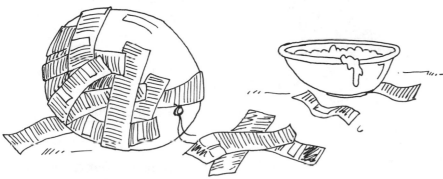

6. Use masking tape to cover the opening.

7. Glue leaves all over the outside of the newspaper-covered balloon. Add flowers or any other natural materials to give a lovely spring look to your piñata.

8. Tie your finished piñata to a tree branch, and hold your "Rites of Spring" party outside under the tree. Your guests will have extra fun searching for good, sturdy sticks to use as they take turns trying to break the piñata.

Eggshell Tulips

What to Use

- blown eggshells
- red and yellow tempera paint
- paint brush
- scissors
- glue
- vase

What to Do

1. Paint some of the blown eggshells red and some yellow. Allow to dry.

2. Use the scissors to poke a tiny hole in the bottom of each egg. Dip one end of each pipe cleaner in glue and insert into the holes to make a stem for each "tulip."

3. Cut out a pointed opening at the top of each egg to finish off your fake tulips.

4. Arrange your tulips in a vase and enjoy a colorful touch of spring.

5. For a whole flower garden, experiment to make other flowers. Glue on paper petals, cut the eggshells in half and scallop, or use many colors of paint to get rainbow hues for buttercups, poppies, or roses.

Fancy Brown Eggs

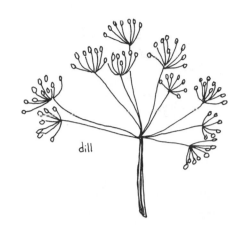

dill

parsley

What to Do

1. Collect some fancy leaves (the lacier the leaves, the prettier your eggs will be). Wash and dry them.

2. Cut the hose or cheese cloth into circles big enough to wrap the eggs in. Cut additional tying strips (see illustration).

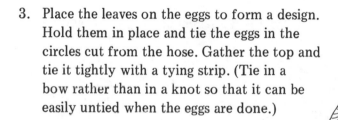

3. Place the leaves on the eggs to form a design. Hold them in place and tie the eggs in the circles cut from the hose. Gather the top and tie it tightly with a tying strip. (Tie in a bow rather than in a knot so that it can be easily untied when the eggs are done.)

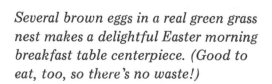

geranium

4. Put the eggs in a pan and cover them with water. Put three or four onion skins in the water.

5. Bring the water to a boil, and simmer the eggs on low heat for fifteen minutes. Remove the pan from the heat and allow to cool in the pan.

6. Unwrap the eggs and admire the lacy white leaf designs on your fancy brown eggs!

What to Use

- eggs
- lacy leaves—grape ivy, geranium, dill, parsley, etc. (Cut tissue paper ones if you can't get real ones.)
- old nylon hose or cheese cloth
- outer skins from an onion
- pan
- water
- hot plate or stove
- adult help

Several brown eggs in a real green grass nest makes a delightful Easter morning breakfast table centerpiece. (Good to eat, too, so there's no waste!)

Natural Tie-Dye Eggs

Using egg dyes from the grocery store is one way to dye Easter eggs. If you really want some naturally dyed eggs for your Easter basket, it'll take a little more time and effort, but you'll get extra special eggs!

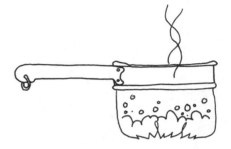

What to Use

To Make the Natural Dyes

- daffodils or crocuses for yellow
- grass, spinach, or moss for green
- tea or coffee grounds for brown
- blueberries or blackberries for blue
- tomatoes for orange
- cranberries for red

And You'll Need

- pot
- strainer
- bowl for each color
- paper towels
- thin cloth
- scissors

What to Do

1. Put your natural materials for one color in a pot with just enough water to cover.

2. Boil them long enough to get the color you want.

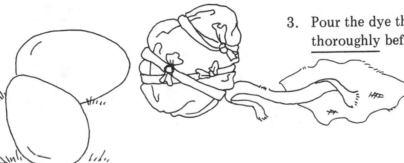

3. Pour the dye through a strainer into a bowl. Then wash the pot thoroughly before you use it to make your next color.

4. Wrap each egg in a piece of cloth. Then cut thin strips of cloth and tie them tightly around the egg in several places.

5. Dip the wrapped eggs in the natural dye and leave them inside the tied cloth to "drip dry" for several hours (overnight is better). You'll be amazed at the beautiful designs you see when you unwrap the eggs!

196

Merry May Baskets

What to Use

- plastic berry baskets
- ribbon or calico strips
- scissors

Surprise your friends and neighbors with baskets of flowers or goodies that you leave secretly on their doorsteps early in the morning on May Day!

What to Do

1. Weave the ribbon or calico strips through the openings in the berry basket. Tie a nice bow.

2. Fill the basket with weeds or hard boiled eggs that you've decorated with natural dyes.

A Solar Celebration!

Plan a solar celebration for a hot, sunny day.
Use this menu and the following recipes for an outdoor brunch.

What to Do

1. Make your jam a day or two before your solar celebration.

2. Get up early on the big day! Prepare the tea according to the recipe
    and set it outside to brew.

3. Prepare the citrus fruit cups and cover them with plastic wrap.

4. Prepare the toast according to the recipe and wrap it
    in plastic wrap.

5. Walk all around your outside space and choose a place to cook.
    Use a sidewalk or concrete patio if at all possible because
    it will hold the sun's heat better and help cook the food
    faster.

6. Place the citrus fruit cups and toast on the sidewalk.
    Prepare the eggs and put them on the sidewalk, too.

7. While waiting for the food to cook,
    prepare the tea, bring out the plates, forks,
    and jam, and entertain your
    guests.

Solar Celebration Menu

Sidewalk fried eggs
Hot citrus fruit cup
Buttered cinnamon toast
Sun berry jam
Solar tea with lemon, sugar,
   and mint
(See recipes.)

HOT CITRUS CUPS

2 tablespoons honey	knife and spoon
1 grapefruit	bowl
1 orange	clear plastic wrap

1. Cut a firm grapefruit and an orange in half.

2. Cut the fruit sections out of both and mix them in a bowl with 1 tablespoon of honey.

3. Put half of the fruit in each grapefruit cup and drizzle a little more honey over each cup.

4. Cut a thin circle and six slivers from the orange rind to decorate the top of each cup with a sun.

5. Cover with plastic wrap and leave these to cook in the sun.

SIDEWALK FRIED EGGS

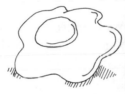

piece of foil wrap	margarine
salt and pepper	2 eggs

1. Grease the foil wrap with the margarine and place it on the hottest spot on the sidewalk.

2. Break the eggs directly onto the foil to cook. (The amount of the sun's heat will determine how fast they cook.)

3. Serve the eggs with salt and pepper.

SOLAR TEA

2 tea bags	mint leaves
lemon	sugar or honey
clean quart jar with a lid	

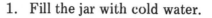

1. Fill the jar with cold water.

2. Put two tea bags in the water and screw the top on the jar.

3. Place the jar in a sunny spot for about three hours.

4. When the tea looks dark enough, take out the tea bags and add some crushed mint leaves if you have them.

5. Serve the tea over ice with lemon and sugar or honey.

BUTTERED CINNAMON TOAST

2 thick slices of bread	cinnamon and sugar
margarine and a spreader	clear plastic wrap

1. Spread the bread with margarine and sprinkle both sides of each piece with cinnamon and sugar.

2. Wrap each slice in clear plastic wrap and place both slices directly on the hot sidewalk.

3. After thirty minutes, turn so that both sides will be toasted.

You wouldn't want to cook breakfast like this every day, but it will be fun once in a while!

Fall Wool-Sock Walk

What to Do

1. Dress warmly and wear good walking shoes. Be sure to put on long wool socks or wool pants (or some other fabric that's very much like wool).

2. Look for a field or yard or woods or an empty lot where there are lots of grasses and weeds.

3. Go for a walk! Wander and roam, looking and listening and smelling and enjoying the fall day. Let your legs brush up against as many bushes and plants and weeds as possible.

4. When your walk is over, take a look at what has stuck to your socks or pants! Carefully pick off each bristle or grass or burr or weed or seed. Look at each one a long time. Can you describe each one? Write some words that tell how each looks and feels.

5. If you'd like to save your collection, glue them to the construction paper. Label the paper with the date and place of your walk.

What to Use

- a crisp fall day
- plenty of time
- wool pants or long wool socks
- a field or forest or empty lot
- glue and construction paper
- a crayon or pencil

Harvest Good Luck Symbols

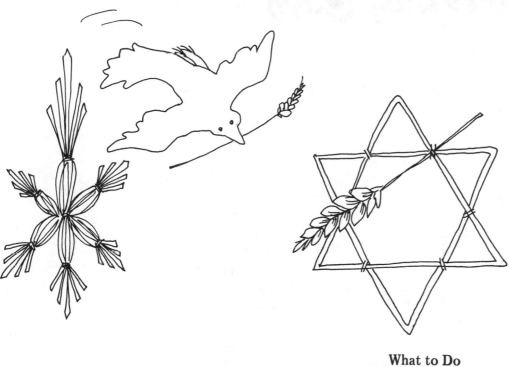

What to Use

- firm stalks of wheat, rye, or sturdy dried grasses
- scissors
- pail
- water
- string

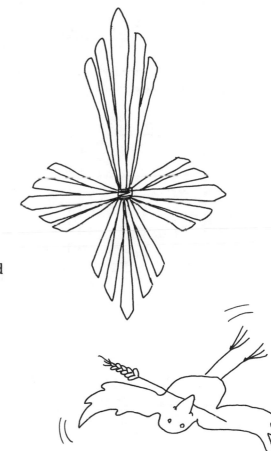

What to Do

1. Soak the stalks in a pail full of water to make them flexible and easy to form into the desired shapes.

2. Cut the stalks into lengths that you find easy to work with. Experiment to make the designs shown here, and shape some of your own.

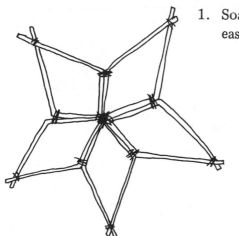

Nutty Place Cards

Get ready for an autumn feast by decorating your table with these nutty place cards!

What to Do

1. Paint each cardboard square green and allow it to dry.

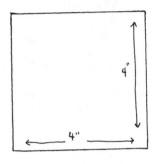

2. Next, roll each cardboard square into a cone and secure it with tape.

What to Use

- 4 inch cardboard squares
- liquid white glue
- tape
- waxed paper
- nuts in shells
- glitter
- berries
- scissors
- green paint
- 1 x 2 inch paper rectangles

3. Cut off the bottom so that the cone will sit flat on the table.

4. Spread out some waxed paper over your work surface and place the cones on it.

5. Start at the bottom and glue nuts and berries all the way around the cone. Let each row dry thoroughly before you start to work on the next one.

6. Write each guest's name on a paper rectangle with glue. Sprinkle lots of glitter over the glue and allow it to dry before shaking off the extra glitter.

7. Make a very small cut in the top of the cone. Place the paper rectangle with the glittered name on it into the slit.

8. Carefully peel your cones away from the waxed paper and take them to your table. Arrange your place cards and get ready to enjoy the autumn feast.

Jewelry fit for a Witch

What to Do

1. Wash the pumpkin seeds and spread them on paper towels or newspapers to dry. (Overnight is better, but an hour or two will do.)

2. Put some pumpkin seeds in each of the two jars. Put a little orange food coloring in one and some black in the other. Add ½ teaspoon of water to each jar.

3. Shake the jars until the seeds are colored.

4. Spread the seeds on paper to dry.

5. String them in several lengths to make witch's jewelry—rings, bracelets, and necklaces. You can twist or braid several strands or wear single strands of many lengths, or use your imagination to create an original design all your own.

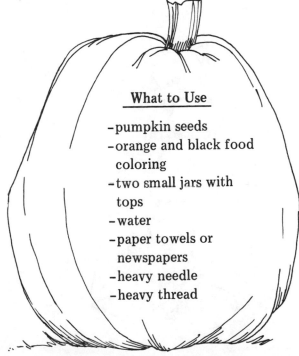

What to Use

- pumpkin seeds
- orange and black food coloring
- two small jars with tops
- water
- paper towels or newspapers
- heavy needle
- heavy thread

A Natural Menorah

What to Do

1. Start looking in the summer for some good mud daubers' nests. You will need nine of the long, tube-like sections, so locate as many nests as you need. Look for them on the sides of buildings or on fences.

2. Wait until the fall or winter when the nests are empty to do your collecting. (A mud dauber's sting is very painful.) Use a flat spatula to pry the nest away from its backing. You might want to ask a grown-up for some help or advice on this part.

What to Use

- mud daubers' nests
- flat spatula
- weathered board
- glue
- picture hanger
- shellac
- candles
- adult help

3. Arrange the nine tube-like sections on the weathered board in a way that pleases you. Put the tops of the tubes above the edge of the wood so the wood will not burn when the candles are lit. Then glue the tubes in place.

4. Attach a picture hanger to the back of the wood.

5. Cover the nests with a coat of shellac so they will not crumble with use.

6. When Chanukah comes, place your candles in the tubes just as you would in a regular Menorah, and celebrate Chanukah "naturally!"

Celebrate Chanukah...with potatoes!

ONE POTATO . . .

For centuries, Jewish children have played many variations of the dreidel game as part of the "Festival of Lights" celebration. Take turns spinning the four-sided top. The one whose top spins longest wins the game.

nun   gimel   hay   shin

What to Use

- felt pen
- sharpened pencil
- potato
- knife

What to Do

1. Cut the two ends off the potato, and trim the remaining portion into a six-sided cube. Make it as square as possible.

2. Use the knife to cut a hole large enough to stick the pencil in all the way through the potato cube.

3. With a felt pen, print one of the above symbols on each of the four sides of the potato.

   These are the first letters in the four Hebrew words that mean "A great miracle happened there."

4. You're now ready to play the dreidel game. While you are spinning your dreidel, use this chant or make up your own.

   Oh, watch my twirling dreidel
   As round and round it spins.
   Which letter will it show me
   When all the turning ends?

TWO POTATO . . .

Print special Chanukah gift wrap paper. If you're going to celebrate properly, you'll need a lot because Jewish children get a present on each of the eight nights of Chanukah—and it's traditional to wrap the gifts in blue and white paper.

What to Use

- two potatoes
- blue tempera paint
- small pie tins or bowls
- white butcher or tissue paper
- knife

What to Do

1. Cut two potatoes in half. Use each half to make a print pattern.

2. Draw a candle with a flame on one potato half, a dreidel on one half, a six-pointed star on another half, and a Hebrew letter on the last one.

3. Use the knife to carve around these drawings so that they become raised shapes.

4. Dip the potato halves in the blue paint and press onto the white paper to make an all-over print design.

5. Make several sheets of this paper so you'll have some to share.

Every true Chanukah menu contains delicious latkes. A latke is really just a potato pancake with a fancy name.

THREE POTATO . . .

What to Use

- bowl
- grater
- spatula

- 3 potatoes
- margarine or oil
- 2 Tbsp. of self-rising flour

- knife
- frying pan
- stove

- 1 egg
- pinch of salt
- cinnamon
- sugar

What to Do

1. Peel and grate the potatoes into a bowl.

2. Add the egg, salt, and flour, and stir.

3. Melt enough margarine (or use oil) in the frying pan to cover the bottom. Let it get very hot.

4. Drop big spoonfuls of the mixture into the pan and fry until they are golden brown on one side. Turn with the spatula to brown the other side.

5. Cook enough for everybody in your family and serve with jam and sour cream. You'll each want at least two or three!

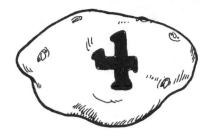

FOUR

Use your last four potatoes to make a Menorah!

-four potatoes
-knife
-modeling clay
-eight small candles
-one large candle
-natural twigs and dried weeds

What to Do

1. Cut the four potatoes in half. Put the cut, flat side down on the table and make a hole in the top of each potato half.

2. Use the modeling clay to form a half circle large enough to hold the eight potato halves.

3. Stick the largest candle into the center of the clay form.

4. Place four potato halves (cut side down) on either side of the candle. Press them into the clay.

5. Stick a candle into each of the potato holders.

6. Decorate the menorah with natural twigs and dried weeds.

Decorate Your Tree Naturally

. . . WITH PINE CONES

What to Use

- pine cones—as many shapes and sizes as possible
- bows and ribbons
- glitter
- beads or buttons
- yarn
- glue
- ornament hooks
- gold or silver paper

1

What to Do

1. Make ribbon loops for hanging.

    OR

2. Randomly dab some glue on the pine cones and sprinkle with glitter.

    OR

3. Braid red and green yarn and tie loops with fat bows.

    OR

5

5. Decorate the cones with gold or silver paper stars and hang with Christmas tree ornament hooks.

    OR

6

3

2

4

4. Glue old beads or buttons to the pine cones and hang them with fishing line or thin threads.

    OR

6. Hang yarn pompoms from the ends of the cones.

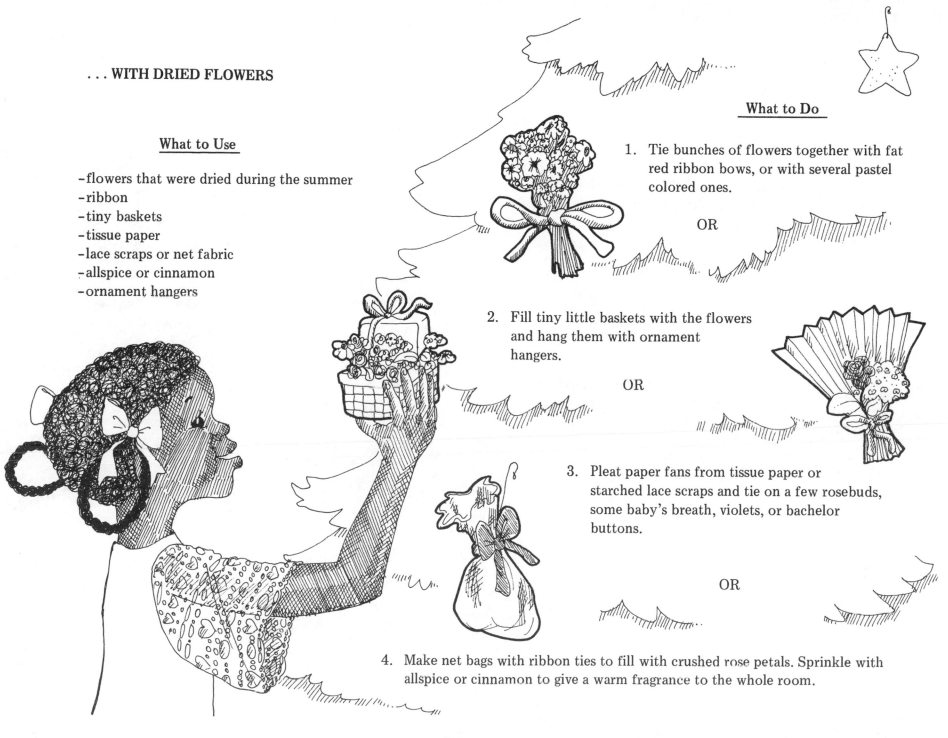

. . . WITH DRIED FLOWERS

What to Use

- flowers that were dried during the summer
- ribbon
- tiny baskets
- tissue paper
- lace scraps or net fabric
- allspice or cinnamon
- ornament hangers

What to Do

1. Tie bunches of flowers together with fat red ribbon bows, or with several pastel colored ones.

    OR

2. Fill tiny little baskets with the flowers and hang them with ornament hangers.

    OR

3. Pleat paper fans from tissue paper or starched lace scraps and tie on a few rosebuds, some baby's breath, violets, or bachelor buttons.

    OR

4. Make net bags with ribbon ties to fill with crushed rose petals. Sprinkle with allspice or cinnamon to give a warm fragrance to the whole room.

. . . WITH POPCORN AND FRUIT

What to Do

1. Make cranberry chains and popcorn chains. If you'd like, add some seeds or buttons.

2. Tie lemons, limes, oranges, and apples with yarn or net strips and hang with ornament hangers.

What to Use

- cranberries
- popcorn
- strong thread and needle
- seeds or buttons
- yarn
- ornament hangers

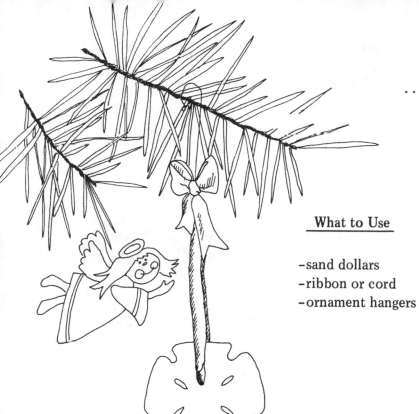

. . . WITH SAND DOLLARS

What to Use

-sand dollars
-ribbon or cord
-ornament hangers

What to Do

1. Collect or buy sand dollars.

2. Wash and dry the sand dollars.

3. Loop ribbon, cord, or tinsel through the natural hole and tie in a tiny bow. Choose ribbon that matches your tree's other decorations.

4. Attach an ornament hanger to each bow and hang the sand dollars on your tree.

213

Milkweed Pod Star

What to Use

- five milkweed seed pods
- pipe cleaners
- acorn cup, half a pecan shell, or a mini-pine cone
- glue

What to Do

1. Glue pipe cleaners to the milkweed seed pods.

2. Arrange the seed pods in a star design. Join the pipe cleaners to hold the seed pods together and fasten them behind the star.

3. Add an extra pipe cleaner to form a hanging loop.

4. Glue the acorn cup, nut shell, or pine cone in the center of the star to cover the connecting ends.

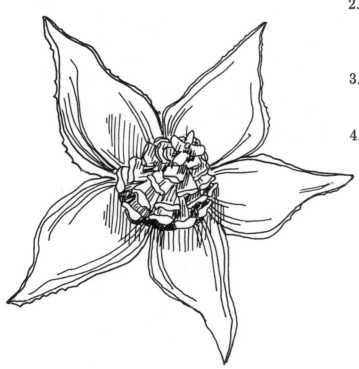

Cone-A-Tree

What to Do

1. Collect a basket full of pine cones that are about the same size and shape.

2. Arrange pine cones around the outer rim of the cardboard circle.

3. Glue the pine cones in place and leave to dry for a few minutes.

4. Place the cardboard or styrofoam cone inside the pine cone ring.

5. Glue the pine cones in rows around the cone. Work carefully to arrange each row to show off the natural beauty of each cone, and also to shape the tree.

6. Decorate the finished tree with miniature pine cones, berries, or seed pod ornaments. A tiny artificial bird may be added for color.

What to Use

- pizza board or cardboard circle
- glue
- cardboard or styrofoam cone

Use this as a centerpiece for your Christmas breakfast!

CORNCOB JELLY for holiday gifts!

Wait!! Don't throw those corncobs away!
You can use them to make delicious,
old fashioned jelly.

What to Use

-knife
-large cooking pot
-bowl
-water
-measuring cup
-tablespoon
-old pillowcase
-jelly jars
-adult help
-these ingredients:
   12 large, dry red corncobs
    3 pints water
    1 package powdered pectin
    3 cups sugar
    1 tablespoon lemon juice

What to Do

1. Wash cobs in cold water and cut them into small pieces.

2. Put them in the pot and cover them with water.
   Boil gently for 35 minutes.

3. Pour the cobs and water into the pillowcase and strain the juice into the bowl. (You may need a grownup's help for this.)

4. Measure three cups of the corn juice and put it back into the pot. (Add some water if you don't have three cups of juice.)

5. Add pectin to the juice and bring it to a boil.

6. Allow this juice to boil two minutes and remove from heat.

7. Pour the mixture into well washed jars.

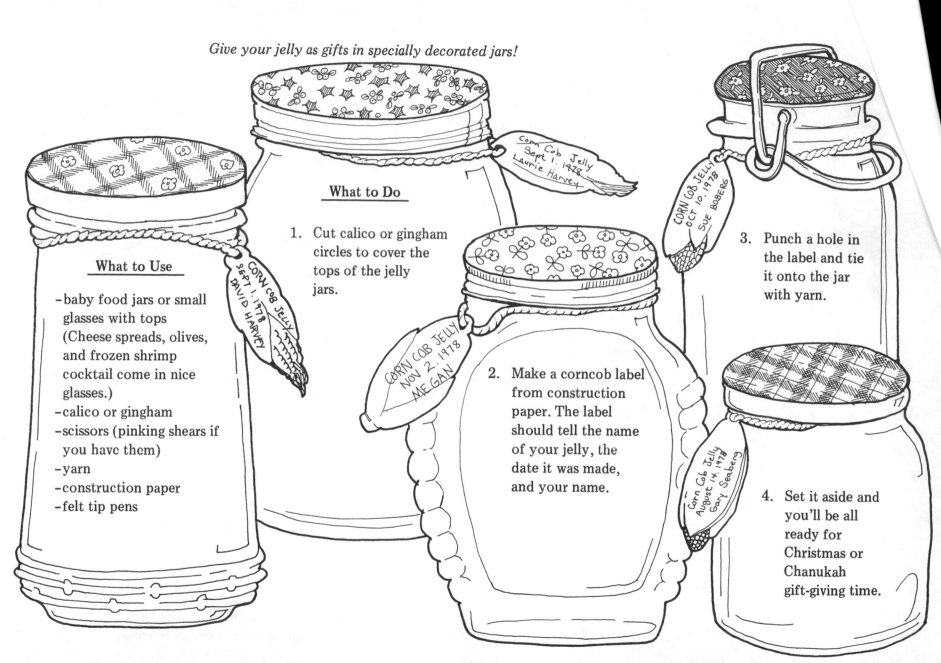

Give your jelly as gifts in specially decorated jars!

What to Do

1. Cut calico or gingham circles to cover the tops of the jelly jars.

2. Make a corncob label from construction paper. The label should tell the name of your jelly, the date it was made, and your name.

3. Punch a hole in the label and tie it onto the jar with yarn.

4. Set it aside and you'll be all ready for Christmas or Chanukah gift-giving time.

What to Use

- baby food jars or small glasses with tops (Cheese spreads, olives, and frozen shrimp cocktail come in nice glasses.)
- calico or gingham
- scissors (pinking shears if you have them)
- yarn
- construction paper
- felt tip pens

217

Bird's Nest Legend

What to Use

- bird's nest
- hair spray
- modeling clay
- tempera paint
- clothespin
- white liquid glue

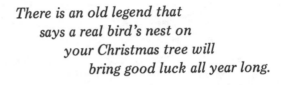

*There is an old legend that
says a real bird's nest on
your Christmas tree will
bring good luck all year long.*

What to Do

1. During the summer and fall, search for a nest for your Christmas tree. Be sure the birds aren't still living in it.

2. Press the sides of the nest together carefully and spray it with hair spray to hold the shape. Glue a clothespin onto the nest so that it can be attached to the tree.

3. You might want to make a few eggs from modeling clay. Paint them with tempera paint before putting them in the nest.

218

a tree for all seasons

What to Do

1. Look for an interesting branch to use for your special tree (try to find a twiggy one). If you go to the woods or a park, you can probably find one on the ground.

What to Use

- interesting branch found on the ground
- scissors
- plastic spoon
- plaster of Paris
- water
- coffee can
- clay flower pot
- ribbon or yarn
- white glue
- decorations to fit the season
- cardboard

2. Mix the plaster of Paris with water in the coffee can. Stir and add more water until the mixture is about as thick as a milkshake.

3. Put a circle of cardboard in the bottom of the pot to cover the hole. Then fill the pot almost to the top with the plaster mixture.

4. Stick the branch in the middle of the mixture and push it down to the bottom of the pot. Hold the branch straight up for a few minutes to give the plaster time to harden.

5. Wrap the ribbon or yarn around the pot and make the prettiest bow you can. (If you use yarn, you may want to make pom-poms.)

6. Select decorations to fit the season. (See the long list of suggestions on the next three pages!)

7. Find a special spot for your Tree For All Seasons and enjoy it all year long.

For noisy New Year's party decorations, tie on horns, clappers, and paper blowers from the dime store.

For Valentine's Day, use red and pink hearts cut from tissue paper and hung with red and pink ribbons. (Glue a red heart and a pink one back-to-back with a ribbon loop glued in-between!)

For St. Patrick's Day, cut green construction paper shamrocks and hang them with white or green pipe cleaners.

For Easter, try decorated eggs (either blown or hard boiled) hung by pastel ribbons.

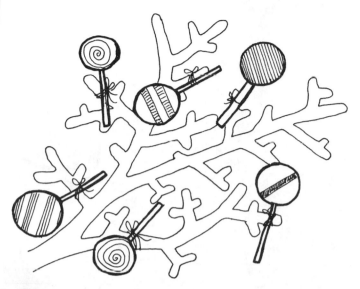

For any party occasion, a lollipop tree,
a candy corn tree, or a trinket tree will add to the
festivities.

For a Trip Tree, cut pictures from post cards, road maps,
and menus, or add some pictures of your own. Cut
pictures into circles, squares, triangles, stars, etc., and
glue two pictures back to back to add interest.
Punch a hole in the top and make a yarn loop for hanging.

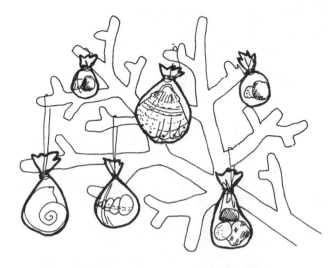

After a beach vacation, cover the shells and shiny pebbles
you collected with plastic wrap and tie them to the branches
with twisted and knotted twine. Add a few small pieces
of driftwood or some seaweed.

After an autumn nature walk, hang acorns, nuts, seed pods,
dried foliage, etc. on the tree with yarn.

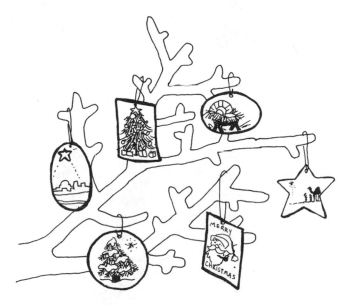

For Christmas, use old greeting cards and whatever you can find around the house—use your imagination!

For Father's Day, wrap homemade cookies in clear plastic and tie on with kitchen twine.

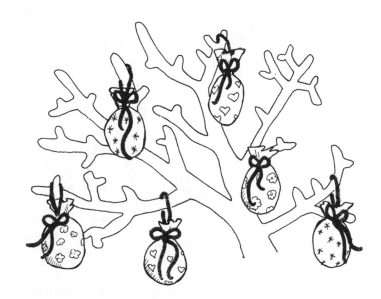

For a Mother's Day gift, make tiny sachets from dried flowers, a drop or two of cologne and some allspice wrapped in net and tied with pastel colored ribbons.

For a grandmother on Grandmother's Day, family snapshots pasted on lace paper doilies and hung with sewing thread would be perfect!

Hurrah for Seasons

WELCOME EACH NEW SEASON with a special celebration!

*Watch your calendar for the first day of the upcoming season and start
planning the festive events a few weeks ahead of time.
Invite friends and neighbors to celebrate with you!*

Your celebration might include such events as:

- a snowball-throwing party
- a good old-fashioned tumble in piles of leaves
- a summer keep-cool party
- skating or snowsliding together, followed by hot cider
- a springtime sunrise breakfast
- a toasty warm winter sunset dinner
- a celebrate-the-sun dance (or celebrate-the-moon, or snow, etc.)
- special solar recipes to stir up
- making snow sculptures
- a hike together through the woods (in any season)
- silly skits about starting the garden (or any other seasonal chores)
- lie-telling about how hot the summer is going to be (or how cold the winter)
- a group rain-walk or a walk through the puddles after a storm
- an autumn feast
- a spring poetry party
- creating songs for the season
- a watermelon-eating contest
- a Rites of Spring party
- a blindfolded fall woods walk
- a leaf-raking tournament
- a spring neighborhood clean-up parade

Hurrah For
Outdoor Folks!

Who's Who Outdoors?

What kinds of folks will you find in the out-of-doors?
Who spends a lot of time out there? How do they feel
about the outdoors? Whenever you're outside, look
around to see who else is out there, too.

What to Use

- notebook and pencil
- Outdoor Autographs sheet (following page)
- book on careers (from your library)
- pen

What to Do

1. When you're outdoors, look at people around you.
   See if you can find people who are working

        playing
        relaxing
        exercising
        going somewhere.

2. Try to get the autographs of as many outdoor folks as possible.
   Use the suggestions on the next page, or design an Autograph
   Sheet of your own.

3. Find a book on careers in your library. Start making a list of
   all the outdoor jobs you learn about.

4. You might try interviewing some outdoor folks.
   Find out: What they're doing.
       How they like working or playing
        outdoors.
       Why the outdoors is important to them.
       How much time they spend outdoors.

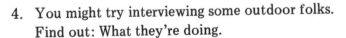

Be sure to interview folks and ask for autographs only if the people are willing to talk to you
and only with your parents' permission.

OUTDOOR AUTOGRAPHS

Someone who works outdoors year round _____

Someone who is walking or feeding an animal _____

A birdwatcher _____

Two kids playing _____

Two grownups playing _____

Someone who works outdoors only in warm weather _____

Someone who is gardening _____

A kid who is working _____

Someone who is cleaning up something _____

Someone who is building something _____

Someone who is fixing something _____

A hiker, camper or backpacker _____

Someone who is cooking _____

Someone who loves being outside in cold weather _____

Someone who loves being outside in the rain _____

A grownup exercising _____

Someone who goes for a walk every day _____

Someone who is taking care of trees or other plants _____

Three people who think we need to take better care of the outdoors _____

Someone who has worked outdoors for more than 10 years _____

A sunbather _____

Someone who is reading _____

Someone who is picking up litter _____

Recycle Trip

Look around your house and neighborhood for the stuff people don't want anymore. A lot of that junk is GOOD JUNK. GOOD JUNK is stuff that shouldn't be thrown away because it has other uses. Set off on a trip to collect some of that GOOD JUNK and give it a second life!

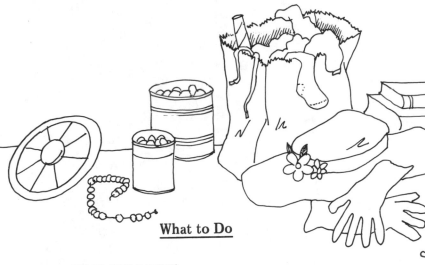

What to Do

1. FIRST YOU COLLECT!

   –Start looking at home first—in drawers, the attic, the garage, the basement.

   –Ask your friends and neighbors for their cast-away junk.

   –Talk to people who work in factories and stores (or visit these places) and ask them for the stuff they throw away. Factories, hardware stores, ice cream stores, wallpaper stores, grocery stores, paint stores, carpet shops, offices, and hospitals are good sources of valuable throw-aways.

   –Hang around after a neighborhood garage sale and ask for some of the stuff that didn't get sold.

What to Use

–cart or wagon or huge box
–friends
–lots of time and imagination

Here are some of the things you might look for:

jugs	*paper and plastic cups*	*coat hangers*	*plastic bottles*
jars	*spools*	*planting pots*	*old shoes*
cans	*clothespins*	*old license plates*	*old clothes*
bottles	*fabric scraps*	*buttons*	*sawdust*
aluminum pie tins	*yarn scraps*	*pieces of games*	*styrofoam packing chips*
styrofoam meat trays	*ribbon*	*wallpaper samples*	*old silverware*
cottage cheese containers	*cardboard tubes*	*carpet scraps*	*magazines*
margarine tubs	*skates*	*linoleum tiles*	*catalogs*
egg cartons	*bicycle wheels*	*nails*	*baskets*
boxes of all sizes	*broken toys*	*string*	*sheets*
crates from large appliances	*tin foil*	*broken balloons*	*pillowcases*
cardboard scraps	*bottle tops*	*popsicle sticks*	*paper bags*
milk cartons	*bottle caps*	*shoeboxes*	*newspapers*
coffee cans	*straws*	*old filmstrips or film*	*mirrors (Not with sharp edges!)*
	mittens or gloves	*hairbrushes*	*pots and pans*
			dishpans
			coat racks
			paint brushes
			paint rollers

2. NEXT, YOU ORGANIZE!

Get friends to help you sort and organize all the GOOD JUNK you've gathered.

Put things that are alike in boxes or bags so you know what you've got.

This way it will be ready to use when you decide what to do with it.

229

3. THEN, YOU RECYCLE!!

Give your GOOD JUNK a new life with any of these ideas and more of your own!

planters
scarecrows
games
art projects
musical instruments
puzzles
holiday crafts
counting toys
cameras
airplanes
dolls
new filmstrips
room organizers
go-carts
mobiles
gifts

puppets
toys
crafts
dress-up costumes
drums
wind chimes
tools for arts and crafts
picture books
weavings
boats
Christmas decorations
puppet theaters
math aids
totem poles
room decorations
hats
scenery for plays

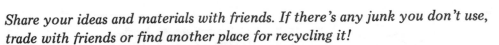

Share your ideas and materials with friends. If there's any junk you don't use, trade with friends or find another place for recycling it!

Litter Brigade...Clean-up Parade

keep it CLEAN!

TAKE ME TO YOUR LITTER!

LITTER BRIGA

CLEAN UP

What to Do

1. Gather some friends to form a Clean-up Parade. Bring wagons, carts, large bags, and boxes for collecting litter.

2. Use the cardboard and markers to make signs to carry or hang on your carts. The signs will identify your group as a Litter Brigade.

3. March along together or split up into groups to cover as much of your neighborhood or school yard or park as possible.

4. Pick up paper, cans, bottles, or other trash that's lying where it doesn't belong. Wear gloves so that you won't get hurt picking up bottles and cans. Be very careful not to touch broken bottles or rusty cans with your bare hands.

5. When your containers are full, meet the rest of the Litter Brigade members and sort out the litter. Separate the paper, cans, glass, and other junk.

6. Try to find recycling centers that will take the glass and the cans you find.

7. Enjoy a cleaner neighborhood!!

What to Use

- heavy gloves
- lots of kids
- wagons, carts, large garbage bags
- cardboard
- markers

As you march along, let people know what you're doing. Maybe this will encourage them to help in the fight against litter!

231

Watching Out for the Outdoors

Who's watching out for your environment? Are you careful not to contribute to damage or pollution of your land, air, and water? How about the folks in your neighborhood?

Here are some Ecology-Checks for you and for the area where you live. How do you rate?

What to Use

-Ecology Checklists (on the next page)
-pencil

What to Do

1. Take a tour of your neighborhood. Repeat this on several days. Each time, watch for the items on the Neighborhood Ecology-Check.

2. After several days of watching, check YES or NO on the list. Count up the YES and NO answers.

3. Get together with your friends and see if you can think of some ideas for helping to turn some or all of the NOs into YES answers.

4. Check yourself on your care of the environment. Use the Personal Ecology-Check on the next page. How do you score? Take a hard look at those NO answers. Try to turn each one into a YES.

NEIGHBORHOOD ECOLOGY-CHECK	YES	NO
Area is usually quiet with little bothersome noise.		
Lights are turned out at night in most houses and buildings.		
Leaves are hauled away or composted instead of burned.		
Very little litter is lying around on ground or in water.		
Citizens keep yards and streets cleaned up.		
Trash can areas are neat.		
Streams, ponds, rivers, or lakes are free of trash or chemicals or oil.		
Many citizens use unleaded gas.		
Many folks ride in car pools.		
Many folks walk or ride bikes instead of driving cars.		
The air is usually free of smoke or dirty particles.		
Poison sprays banned in the area.		
Many folks show concern for the environment.		

PERSONAL ECOLOGY-CHECK	YES	NO
I remember not to litter.		
I save or recycle newspaper.		
I turn off the water while I'm washing or brushing my teeth.		
I save or recycle egg cartons.		
I use both sides of drawing paper and writing paper.		
I return bottles to the store.		
I recycle glass and aluminum.		
I am careful to turn off lights.		
I re-use plastic bags, lunch bags, wrapping paper.		
I walk or bike places instead of riding in a car.		
I take short showers.		
I use paper towels, toilet paper, and tissues sparingly.		
I try to read and learn all I can about ecology.		
I help to keep my neighborhood clean.		

233

Recycled Footwear

What to Use

- old tire
- old innertube
- matt knife or very heavy scissors
- carpet tacks
- chalk
- scissors
- hammer
- paper and pencil
- adult helper

What to Do

1. Use the paper to make a pattern for the sole of your sandals. Draw around your LEFT and RIGHT feet. Make the sole a little bigger than each foot. Cut out the pattern.

2. Place the patterns on the tire and trace around them with chalk. Use the matt knife to cut out the two soles. BE VERY CAREFUL! You should ask an adult to help you with the cutting.

3. Cut four strips from the innertube. Each strip should be long enough to reach from the bottom edge of the sole by your ankle OVER your foot to the bottom edge of the sole by your toes.

4. Arrange two straps in a criss-cross on each sandal. Fasten the straps to the edges of the soles by hammering carpet tacks in tightly.

Your sandals are ready to wear—even on rough or wet surfaces!

Nature Lover's T-Shirt

Make a T-shirt to show the whole world that you love nature!

What to Do

1. Cut letters from paper to say NATURE LOVER.

2. Spread your newspapers on the floor.

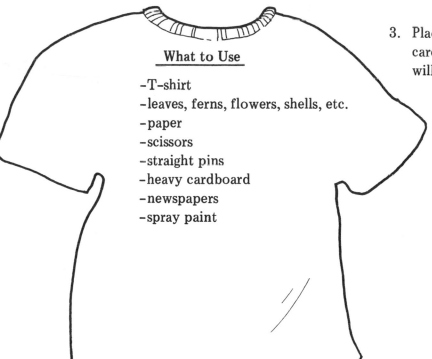

What to Use

-T-shirt
-leaves, ferns, flowers, shells, etc.
-paper
-scissors
-straight pins
-heavy cardboard
-newspapers
-spray paint

3. Place the T-shirt on the newspapers. Flatten the T-shirt out carefully and slip the heavy cardboard inside the T-shirt (this will keep the paint from seeping through the shirt).

4. Place your letters and leaves, flowers, ferns, etc. on the T-shirt. Work until you get a design you like. Pin the design in place.

5. Spray the paint gently over the pinned letters and natural materials. Be very careful to spray just around the materials because too much paint will spoil your design.

6. Let the paint dry before removing letters and other materials.

Run for Your Life

Running is a good activity for keeping your heart and the muscles around your lungs strong. It is important for everyone to keep his heart and lungs in good working order! You can do this by making running (or jumproping, walking, bicycling, or swimming) part of your routine almost every day. Follow these rules when you get ready to run.

What to Use

-running shoes
-loose, comfortable clothes

What to Do

1. Get a pair of running shoes before you start. Running shoes have soft sides and cushioned soles.

2. Always do warm-up exercises before you run. (See the next page.) You can use some of these as cool-down exercises after your run.

3. Try to run at least 3 times a week. Each time you should run 15 minutes or longer. It takes this long for your heart to get working hard enough to begin to increase its strength.

4. Start slowly. Gradually work up to faster running and longer distances. If you feel tired or get any pains, stop and walk for a while. NEVER push till it hurts.

5. Run with a friend sometimes. You should be able to talk while you run unless you're pushing too hard.

6. Run on grass or a track if you can. Choose safe places to run, and run during the daytime.

7. Change your path sometimes so you don't get bored.

238

WARM-UP EXERCISES FOR RUNNERS

Spend 10 minutes warming up before you run, walk, jog, swim, jump rope, or ride your bike.

TOE TOUCH

Stand with your feet wide apart. Bend from the waist and reach toward your left toes with your right hand, then toward your right toes with your left hand. Reach until you feel a slight pull. Hold as you count to 10. Repeat 3 times on each side.

WALL STRETCH

Stretch your right leg straight out and put your foot against a wall at waist level. Then slowly reach toward the wall with your right arm. Reach just until you feel the pull. Hold and count to 10. Repeat 3 times with each leg.

CALF STRETCH

Stand 2 feet away from the wall. With your arms stretched out, put your hands against the wall. Slowly bend your elbows and lean forward toward the wall. Lean just until you feel a pull in your lower legs. Hold in that position and count to 10 slowly. Repeat 3 times.

KNEE HUG

Lie on your back with both legs stretched out straight. Pull your left knee toward your chest and hug it with both arms. Hold the leg for a count of 10. Then stretch the leg out and hug the right knee. Repeat 3 times with each knee.

TOES TO YOUR NOSE

Sit on the floor with your legs stretched out in front of you and your back straight. Gently point your toes toward your nose. Pull them toward you as far as you can without feeling a strain. Hold for a count of 10. Repeat 3 times.

JUMPING JACKS

Start with your hands at your sides and your feet together. As you jump to spread your feet apart, bring your hands over your head and clap. Return hands to sides and bring your feet back together. Repeat 10 times.

A Dance

What to Use

- comfortable clothes
- soft grass or a mat
- sunny day

1. Face the sun. Stand quietly with your body relaxed and hands at your sides. Breathe IN and OUT slowly.

2. Breathe IN slowly through your nose as you raise your arms up toward the sun. Keep raising your arms up over your head and lean your head and arms back.

3. Slowly breathe OUT as you bend forward and touch your hands to the ground.

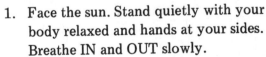

4. Keep your hands on the ground and slowly lower your body to the ground with your left leg straight out behind you and your right knee bent to your chest. Keep your face toward the sun and breathe IN while you're doing this.

5. Bring your right leg out next to your left leg as you breathe OUT. Hold in this position and breathe IN and OUT and IN.

6. Slowly lower your body to the ground with your head down. Breathe OUT.

to Celebrate the Sun

7. Use your arms to push the upper part of your body up from the ground. Raise your head high up toward the sun and breathe IN.

8. As you breathe OUT, push your bottom high up into the air. Lower your head. Breathe IN and OUT and IN and OUT slowly while you hold this position.

9. Breathe IN as you lower your bottom back to the ground and bring your right knee up to your chest.

10. Stand up leaving your body bent at the waist with your hands reaching toward the floor. Breathe OUT as you do this movement.

11. Raise your hands and arms up toward the sun as you breathe IN. Bend your head back.

12. Breathe OUT as you slowly return to your starting position with hands relaxed at your sides. Breathe IN and OUT slowly 5 times as you relax.

Relax Like A Jellyfish

Let the animals give you a lesson in unwinding and relaxing. Watch animals whenever you can and mimic some of them to help you relax and stretch your body.

What to Use

- your body
- soft surface outdoors or indoors
- quiet surroundings
- comfortable clothing

What to Do

1. Try each animal position. Move into each position slowly and smoothly.

2. NEVER stretch your muscles until they hurt. Stretch only until you feel a slight pull, then hold the position as you count to 10 slowly.

3. Breathe IN through your nose and OUT through your mouth slowly as you hold a position.

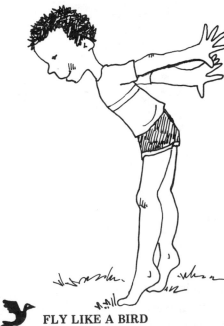

 **STRETCH LIKE A CAT**

Start on your hands and knees with your back straight. Slowly raise your back up high and hold. Lower your back until it is straight.

FLY LIKE A BIRD

Start with your hands at your sides. Slowly lift them up behind you as high as you can. Bend your head forward. Hold, then relax in standing position.

YAWN LIKE A LION

Sit on your feet with hands on your knees. Lean forward on your knees as you open your eyes and mouth very wide. Stick your tongue out as far as you can. Hold. Roar if you wish. Relax and sit back up.

BALANCE LIKE A STORK

Stand very straight. Slowly bring one foot up behind you and balance on the other foot. Hold, then relax with your foot back on the ground. Repeat, bending the other leg.

SIT LIKE A FROG

Sit on the floor with knees bent out and the bottoms of your feet touching each other. Grab hold of your feet and pull them in toward your body. Gently press your knees toward the floor. Keep your back straight and hold.

KNEEL LIKE A CAMEL

Kneel on the ground. Rest your right hand on your right heel, then your left hand on your left heel. Raise your chest up, bend your head back, and hold. Return to kneeling position and rest.

POSE LIKE A COBRA

Lie on your tummy with hands at your sides. Slowly raise your head and bring your hands up under your chin. Push up on your hands to bring your head up and back. Push up until your arms are straight. Hold, then relax.

RELAX LIKE A JELLYFISH

Lie on the ground on your back. Close your eyes. Relax every part of your body. Pretend that you are made of jelly. Breathe in and out slowly for several minutes.

Snacks to Take Along

What to Do

1. Pack up a snack to take along on your next scavenger hunt, hike, bike ride, or walk. Choose from any of these ideas or create take–along snacks of your own!

2. Pack dry snacks in paper bags. Wrap anything that is wet or gooey in foil or a plastic bag.

3. If you're taking juicy fruit slices or salads or anything with a lot of liquid, pack it in a plastic container with a tight lid.

4. Enjoy your outdoor eating!

What to Use

- ingredients for any of the snacks below
- paper or plastic bags or foil
- plastic containers with lids
- spoons or toothpicks

popcorn
nuts and seeds
hardboiled eggs
sticks of celery
carrot
cucumber
zucchini

OTHER SNACKS TO CARRY ALONG

pickles
dried fruit
fresh fruit slices or chunks
cookies
cheese and crackers
meat and cheese kabobs
crackerjack
granola

APPLE–CHEESEWICHES

Slice rings from an apple. Slice pieces of your favorite cheese. Place a slice of cheese between two apple rings for a delightfully different sandwich!

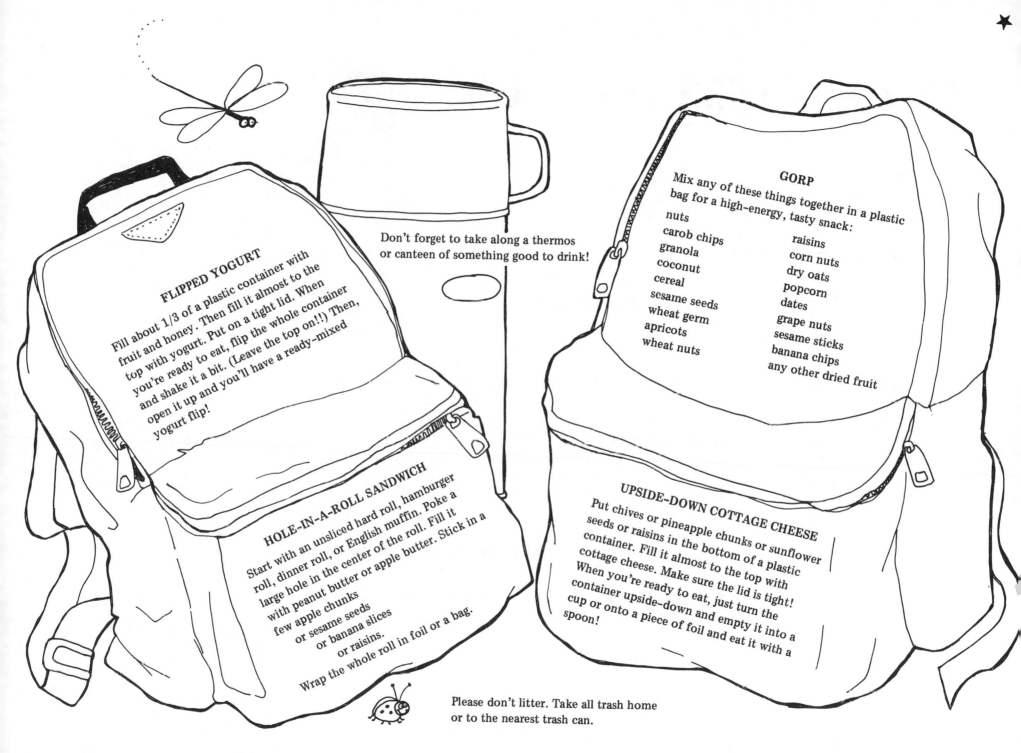

FLIPPED YOGURT

Fill about 1/3 of a plastic container with fruit and honey. Then fill it almost to the top with yogurt. Put on a tight lid. When you're ready to eat, flip the whole container and shake it a bit. (Leave the top on!!) Then, open it up and you'll have a ready-mixed yogurt flip!

HOLE-IN-A-ROLL SANDWICH

Start with an unsliced hard roll, hamburger roll, dinner roll, or English muffin. Poke a large hole in the center of the roll. Fill it with peanut butter or apple butter. Stick in a few apple chunks
or sesame seeds
or banana slices
or raisins.
Wrap the whole roll in foil or a bag.

Don't forget to take along a thermos or canteen of something good to drink!

GORP

Mix any of these things together in a plastic bag for a high-energy, tasty snack:

nuts
carob chips
granola
coconut
cereal
sesame seeds
wheat germ
apricots
wheat nuts

raisins
corn nuts
dry oats
popcorn
dates
grape nuts
sesame sticks
banana chips
any other dried fruit

UPSIDE-DOWN COTTAGE CHEESE

Put chives or pineapple chunks or sunflower seeds or raisins in the bottom of a plastic container. Fill it almost to the top with cottage cheese. Make sure the lid is tight! When you're ready to eat, just turn the container upside-down and empty it into a cup or onto a piece of foil and eat it with a spoon!

Please don't litter. Take all trash home or to the nearest trash can.

245

HURRAH for CORN-ON-THE-COB!

What to Do

1. Pull the husks and silk off the corn.

2. Bring a big pot of water to boil and add a tablespoon of sugar.

What to Use

- corn-on-the-cob
- big pot
- water
- sugar
- salt
- butter

3. Drop the corn into the pot and boil it until tender (about 10 minutes).

4. Serve the corn with plenty of butter and salt.

—OR—

1. Carefully pull the husks back just far enough to remove the silk.

2. Slather some butter on the corn, and pull the husks back up around the ear.

3. Roast on the edge of the fire or grill until tender.

246

Granola Goes Anywhere

GRRREAT GRANOLA

3 cups oatmeal (uncooked)
1 cup nuts (any kind or any mixture of kinds)
½ cup sunflower seeds
¼ cup sesame seeds (optional)
½ cup wheat germ
½ cup raisins
½ cup other dried fruit (optional)
½ cup molasses or honey
½ cup vegetable oil
2 tsp. cinnamon
½ cup shredded coconut (optional)

What to Use

- granola recipe
- ingredients for recipe
- large bowl
- cookie sheet with sides
- measuring spoons
- measuring cups
- large spoon
- oven
- adult help
- container with tight lid

What to Do

1. Mix all the dry ingredients (except raisins and other dried fruit) in a large bowl.

2. Add the honey and oil and stir well until all the dry ingredients are coated.

3. Spread the mixture on a cookie sheet and place in 300° oven for about ½ hour. Stir the mixture often.

4. After you take it out of the oven, stir in the raisins and other dried fruit. Let the mixture cool completely.

5. Store in a tight container.

Enjoy granola dry, with milk, on ice cream, on pudding, on yogurt, on cottage cheese, or on sandwiches!

Carry-Out Caramel Corn

1 cup maple syrup   1 cup brown sugar
½ cup water   ¼ tsp. salt
1 tsp. vanilla   2 T butter
5 cups popped corn   2 cups peanuts
     1½ cups thin pretzel sticks

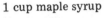

What to Use

- measuring cups and spoons
- wooden stirring spoon
- pan with a handle
- bowl
- cup of cold water
- stove, hot plate, or campfire
- waxed paper
- construction paper
- transparent tape
- recipe and ingredients

What to Do

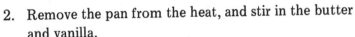

1. Put syrup, sugar, salt, and water in the pan and boil until a half spoonful of the mixture will form a soft ball when dropped in water.

2. Remove the pan from the heat, and stir in the butter and vanilla.

3. Mix the popcorn, peanuts and pretzel sticks in a large bowl. Pour the syrup over the mixture and stir with the wooden spoon until each piece is well coated.

4. Spread the pieces on waxed paper to dry.

5. Roll up construction paper cones and tape them together. Fill the cones with caramel corn and you've made a great treat for a backyard circus or school carnival!

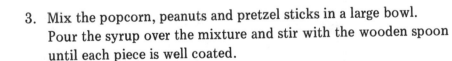

248

Hurrah For
Wind
&
Water
&
Weather!

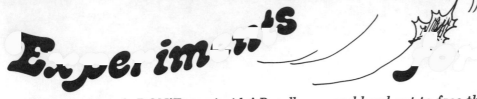

Experiments for a Windy Day

The next time the wind howls DON'T stay inside! Bundle up—and head out to face the wind!

What to Do

1. LISTEN! ! Try to hear all the different sounds that the wind makes. Listen to the way it sounds as it blows through trees or past buildings. Try to imitate the sounds of the wind. Capture some of the sounds on tape if you can.

2. WATCH! ! What does the wind do? Look at the trees, bushes, people walking. Watch how the wind changes things. Hold out a piece of notebook paper. Let it go and measure the distance that the wind carried it. Can the wind blow your hat off? What things do you see blowing around in the wind?

4. LEAN INTO THE WIND!!
Will the wind hold you up?
Turn around. Does the wind push you along?

What to Use

- watch or stopwatch
- measuring tape or measuring stick
- lightweight hat
- notebook paper
- bat and ball
- portable tape recorder (if possible)
- friend

3. SHOUT INTO THE WIND! ! Have a friend stand about 100 feet away from you and shout to her. (Have her stand so that your voice will go <u>with</u> the wind.) Can she hear? Now have her shout back to you (<u>against</u> the wind). Which way can you hear farther—with the wind or against the wind? Measure the distance you can hear each way.

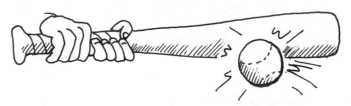

5. BAT INTO THE WIND! ! Try batting a ball <u>with</u> the wind. Measure the distance it flies. Now bat <u>against</u> the wind. How far does it go?

Which Wind!

Many years ago, Sir Francis Beaufort developed this Wind Scale that names and describes different speeds of winds. You can use this scale any day to help you decide what kind of a wind is moving around in the air above you.

What to Use

- Beaufort's Wind Scale
- notebook and pencil

BEAUFORT WIND SCALE			
Number	Name	Effect	Speed mph
0	Calm	Smoke rises vertically	Less Than 1
1	Light air	Smoke drifts	1–3
2	Light breeze	Leaves rustle	4–7
3	Gentle breeze	Flags fly	8–12
4	Moderate breeze	Dust & paper blow	13–18
5	Fresh breeze	Small trees sway	19–24
6	Strong breeze	Hard to use umbrellas	25–31
7	Moderate gale	Hard to walk	32–38
8	Fresh gale	Twigs break off trees	39–46
9	Strong gale	Slight damage to roofs	47–54
10	Whole gale	Trees uprooted	55–63
11	Storm	Widespread damage	64–75
12	Hurricane	Devastation	Above 75

What to Do

1. Watch what the wind does.

2. Check Beaufort's Wind Scale to see if you can identify today's wind. Write the date and name of the wind in your notebook.

3. Try to estimate the speed of the wind.

4. Listen to the weather report to get more information about what the wind is doing. See how the weather report compares to your description of the day's wind.

Who Can Hear The Wind??

Hang up some wind chimes so the wind can make music outside YOUR door!

START WITH NAILS . . .

What to Use

- nylon sewing thread
- large nails of any thickness
- dowel or other thin, sturdy wood
- scissors
- heavy twine
- hook for hanging chimes

What to Do

1. Tie nylon thread around the top of each of several nails.

2. Hang the nails along the dowel. Tie them close enough together so that they will bang against each other when they move.

3. Tie one long piece of twine to the ends of the dowel for a hanger.
   Hang the nail chimes on a porch or in a tree or an open window.

OR, HANG UP SOME JAR LIDS . . .

What to Use

-circle of heavy cardboard
-several canning jar lids with open centers
-thin twine
-nail
-enamel paints and brush (optional)

What to Do

1. Use the nail to poke holes about an inch apart in several places on the cardboard circle.
   The holes should be just a little bigger than the twine. Poke a little larger hole right in the center.

2. Put a double piece of twine through the center hole (from top to bottom).
   Tie a large knot at the bottom to hold the twine to the cardboard.
   This will be the hanger for the chimes.

3. Cut pieces of twine that are about the same length. Thread each one up through a hole and tie a good knot on top of the cardboard.

4. At the end of each string, securely tie a jar lid. (You may paint the lids before doing this if you'd like bright colored wind chimes.)

5. You're ready to hang the chimes in a place where a breeze often blows.

. . . OR, MAKE MUSIC WITH SHELLS!

What to Use

- small piece of driftwood
- 10 of your favorite sea shells
- sand-colored twine
- clear-drying glue
- cup hook
- ceiling hook or nail

Next time you visit the ocean, find a piece of driftwood and collect some shells. With these you can make "Ocean Motion" wind chimes.

What to Do

1. Wash the shells and driftwood thoroughly and let them dry.

2. Cut the twine into equal lengths (one for each shell). The pieces of twine should be long enough to tie around the driftwood with eight inches or so left over.

3. Glue a shell to one end of each piece of twine. Set the shells aside to let the glue dry overnight.

4. When the glue is dry, loop the other end of each piece of twine around the driftwood and tie a knot. Measure carefully so that each shell hangs the same distance from the driftwood.

5. Screw a cup hook into the top of the driftwood. Then hang your "Ocean Motion" wind chimes from a ceiling hook or a nail by a window, and enjoy listening to the shells make music in the wind.

What Do Clouds Know?

What to Use

-Cloud Chart
-notebook and pencil
-book about clouds

What to Do

1. Read the Cloud Chart to get familiar with these four general types of clouds.

2. On the next cloudy day, see if you can identify the kinds of clouds in the sky. Keep a record in your notebook of the date and description of the clouds. Write down your prediction of what the weather might be the next day or later that day. Make a note telling if your prediction was correct.

3. Get a book on clouds from your library. It will help you learn even more about what clouds know!

Clouds can tell you a lot about what's going on up there in the atmosphere. Get to know these kinds of clouds. Use them to help you make your own weather predictions.

CLOUD CHART

Cirrus	-high clouds—20,000 feet or more -feathery wisps or curls -move very rapidly -can be a storm warning
Cumulus	-4000–5000 feet -puffy heaps or domes -many thick ones may become thunderclouds
Stratus	-2000–7000 feet -often are low clouds -foggy, spread out appearance -many spread in flat layers may mean bad weather ahead
Nimbus	-low clouds—1800 feet or so -dark grey, spread widely over sky -these are rain clouds

Easy-to-Do Weather Vane

What to Use

- block of wood
- sturdy drinking straw
- wooden spool
- aluminum foil
- scissors
- glue
- masking or adhesive tape
- heavy cardboard
- compass (for telling directions)
- permanent marker

What to Do

1. Glue the spool to the center of the wood block.

2. Mark NORTH, SOUTH, EAST, WEST at four equal spaces around the bottom of the spool. Go back and write NORTHEAST between NORTH and EAST. Also mark NORTHWEST, SOUTHEAST and SOUTHWEST.

3. Cut a rooster shape and an arrow from heavy cardboard. Or, cut any other animal or shape you'd like. Cover the shape and arrow completely with aluminum foil.

4. Tape the rooster to the top of the straw and tape the arrow below the rooster.

5. Place the straw inside the spool.

6. Set the weather vane outside in a spot where it will catch the wind. Use the compass to find NORTH, and place the weathervane with the word NORTH facing NORTH.

7. Watch the weather vane carefully each day and decide where the wind is coming from. REMEMBER: a wind is named according to the direction from which it blows!

256

hang out a windsock

Some airports use a windsock to tell airplanes the wind direction. This helps the pilots know where the wind is coming from when they're preparing to land their planes. Hang out a windsock in your yard to keep you informed about the wind direction. It will help when you're ready for flying paper planes.

What to Use

-thin net-like fabric
  (cheesecloth or nylon stocking)
-thin wire about 15 inches long
-thick stick
-block of wood (optional)
-nail and hammer
-needle and thread
-twine or string
-scissors
-permanent marker
-compass

What to Do

1. First make the sock. Cut a piece of fabric as wide as the wire is long and about two feet long. Cut the long edges on a slant as shown. Sew the two long edges together.

2. Bend the wire into a circle. Wrap the ends together to hold it in a circle.

3. Sew the biggest end of the sock to the wire.

4. Cut four pieces of string the same length. Attach these at four places around the circle.

5. Pound a nail into the top of the stick. Tie the four strings on the sock around the nail.

6. Nail the stick to the wood block or plant it right into the ground in a place where it will catch the wind.

7. Use a compass to help you mark the directions on the ground or on the board. Watch the windsock each day to tell the wind direction. Remember, a wind is named for the direction from which it <u>comes</u>.

A Simple Anemometer

What to Use

- large, sturdy wood stick (about 2 feet long)
- 2 ping pong balls (or small rubber balls)
- sharp knife
- 2 sturdy, thin sticks of wood (15–20 inches long)
- 4 small nails
- 2 large nails
- enamel paint and brush
- wood block
- hammer
- drill and adult help
- candle

Find out HOW FAST the wind is blowing with this anemometer that you can make yourself!

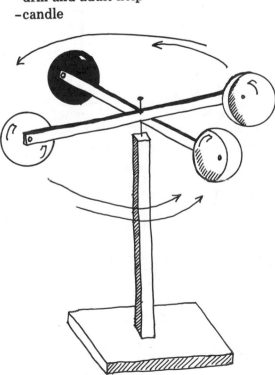

What to Do

1. Drill a hole in one end of the large stick. The hole should be just slightly larger than the pointed end of the large nail.

2. Use one large nail to attach the wood block to the other end of the large stick.

3. Cut the two balls in half with the sharp knife. Paint one of the four balls with a bright color enamel paint. When the paint is dry, nail one ball half to each end of the small sticks. (Use small nails.)

4. Use the other large nail to join the two shorter sticks in the center. Pound the nail through so that half of it extends below the sticks.

5. Stick the sharp end of this nail into the candle so that it is covered with wax.

6. Carefully set this nail into the hole that was drilled at the top end of the large stick. The nail should turn easily in the hole.

7. Hold your anemometer outside a car window while someone is driving 10 miles per hour. Count the number of times that it turns completely around in one minute. (The one colored half will make it easier to count.)

8. Once you know how many times it turns per minute at 10 m.p.h., you can find what the revolutions (the number of times it turns completely around) would be for ONE m.p.h. if you divide by 10.

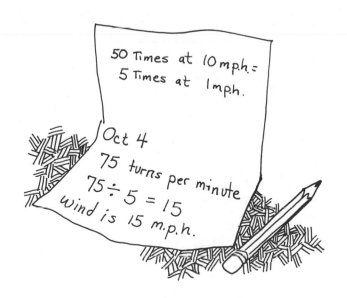

50 Times at 10 m.p.h. = 5 Times at 1 m.p.h.

Oct 4
75 turns per minute
75 ÷ 5 = 15
wind is 15 m.p.h.

9. Now you're ready to measure the speed of the wind. Set the anemometer outside in a spot where it will catch the wind. Count the number of revolutions in a minute. Divide that by the number you found for ONE m.p.h. in your car test. This will tell you today's wind speed.

Investigations into a Mud Puddle

Did you ever pay really close attention to a mud puddle after a good, hard rain? You just might be surprised at who you find living there!

What to Do

1. After a heavy rain, find the largest mud puddle you can. Lie down or squat close beside the puddle and look into it without disturbing the water. What do you see???

2. Look for small animals
     stones
     dirt
     rocks
     grasses.

3. Take a sample of the water by gently dipping your jar into the puddle. Examine the sample with your magnifying glass.

4. Wait a half hour or until the dirt settles and the water in the jar clears. Examine the sample again. What do you notice about the water? Are there any creatures swimming around? What kind of dirt settled out?

5. Of course . . . before you leave the mud puddle, definitely DO take off your shoes and splash and splatter for awhile!

What to Use

−mud puddles
−small glass jar
−magnifying glass

Mud Puddle Paintings

What to Use

- old clothes
- mud
- fingers and toes and sticks
- water supply
- sidewalk
- friends

What to Do

1. After a rainstorm, find a mud puddle or other good, muddy spot. OR make mud by mixing dirt and water. (But DON'T dig up someone's yard!)

2. Use your toes and fingers (and sticks, too) to create mud paintings and sculptures on a sidewalk. If you don't have a sidewalk, you could paint on a wall or porch. GET PERMISSION FIRST!

3. Try handprints, footprints, three-dimensional shapes, mountains and designs.

4. When you're done creating and admiring your artwork, wash it away with a hose or with buckets of water.

5. Clean yourself up before going inside!

261

BUBBLES...BUBBLES...BUBBLES

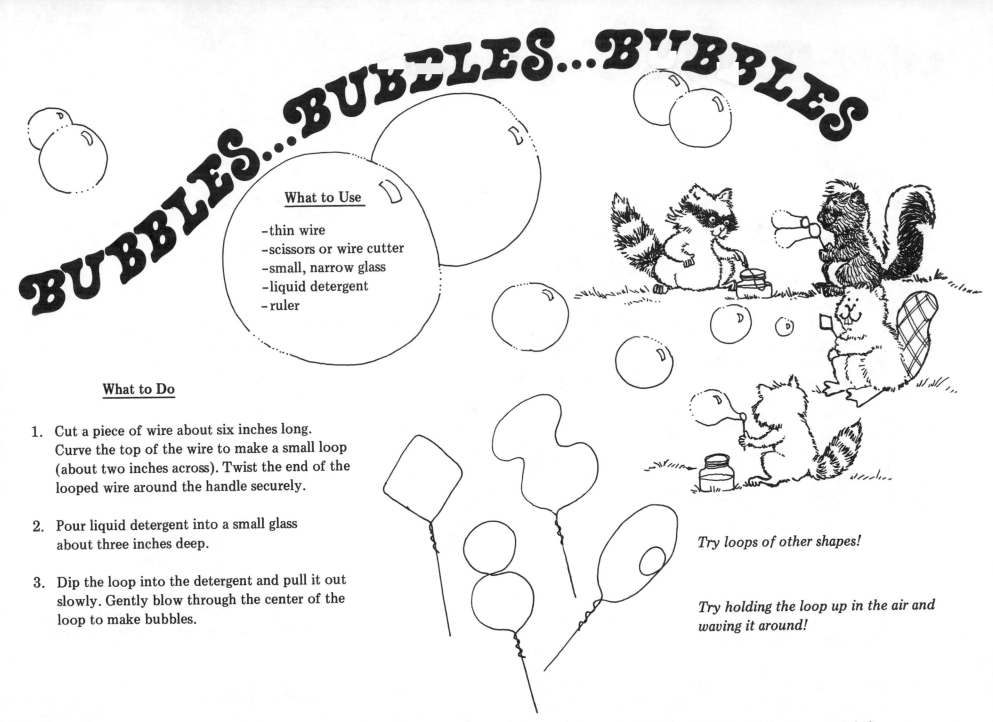

What to Use

- thin wire
- scissors or wire cutter
- small, narrow glass
- liquid detergent
- ruler

What to Do

1. Cut a piece of wire about six inches long. Curve the top of the wire to make a small loop (about two inches across). Twist the end of the looped wire around the handle securely.

2. Pour liquid detergent into a small glass about three inches deep.

3. Dip the loop into the detergent and pull it out slowly. Gently blow through the center of the loop to make bubbles.

Try loops of other shapes!

Try holding the loop up in the air and waving it around!

For a stronger bubble solution, add some glycerine (from the pharmacy) or leave the detergent in the refrigerator overnight!

You Can Make Rainbows

Rainbows occur naturally on a cloudy day when the sun shines at just the right angle through a certain concentration of water drops. You can make rainbows almost any sunny day.

45°

What to Use

−hose with spray nozzle
−sunshine
−friend

What to Do

1. Stand so that the sun is behind you. Have a friend use a hose to spray a fine mist in front of you.

2. Position yourself so that you are looking at the spray at a 45−degree angle. (See the illustration.) You should be able to see the rainbow's colors.

3. Try this experiment at different times of the day until you get the best results.

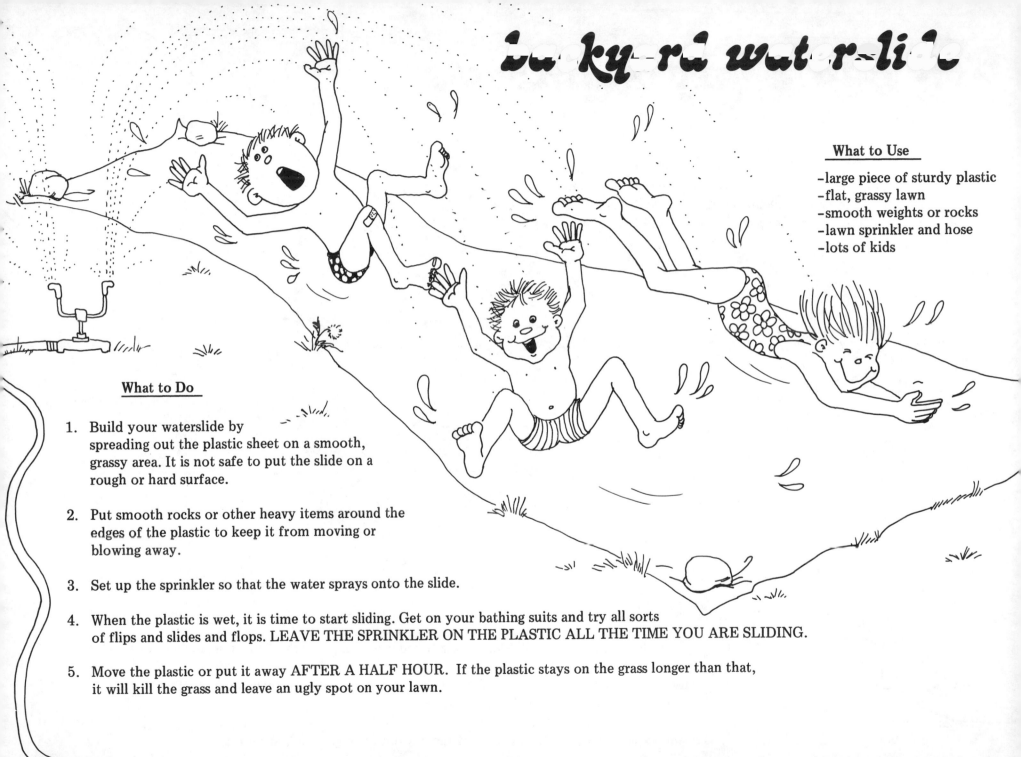

Backyard Water-Slide

What to Use

- large piece of sturdy plastic
- flat, grassy lawn
- smooth weights or rocks
- lawn sprinkler and hose
- lots of kids

What to Do

1. Build your waterslide by spreading out the plastic sheet on a smooth, grassy area. It is not safe to put the slide on a rough or hard surface.

2. Put smooth rocks or other heavy items around the edges of the plastic to keep it from moving or blowing away.

3. Set up the sprinkler so that the water sprays onto the slide.

4. When the plastic is wet, it is time to start sliding. Get on your bathing suits and try all sorts of flips and slides and flops. LEAVE THE SPRINKLER ON THE PLASTIC ALL THE TIME YOU ARE SLIDING.

5. Move the plastic or put it away AFTER A HALF HOUR. If the plastic stays on the grass longer than that, it will kill the grass and leave an ugly spot on your lawn.

Icicle Ice Cream

What to Use

- short, fat aluminum can
- paper cup (taller than the can)
- spoon
- icicles
- box of table salt
- aluminum foil
- rubber band
- milk, cream or half and half
- sugar or honey
- vanilla
- mittens or gloves

What to Do

1. Pick thin icicles from your roof. Keep them in the freezer until you need them.

2. Fill the paper cup a little more than half full of milk or half and half. Stir in a tiny pinch of salt, a few drops of vanilla and a spoon of honey or sugar.

3. Cover the cup tightly with foil and put a rubber band around the top to hold the foil. Set the cup in the center of the can.

4. Put on your gloves and break the icicles into small pieces. Put a layer of icicle pieces into the can around the paper cup.

5. Generously sprinkle salt over the layer of ice. Add another layer of icicle chips and another layer of salt. Keep layering until the ice reaches the top of the can.

6. Take the foil off the cup and stir the milk mixture vigorously with the spoon. Keep stirring for a long time. The mixture will begin to harden into soft ice cream.

7. If the ice melts very much, add more layers of ice and salt.

8. When the ice cream is ready, take out the cup and enjoy the tasty flavor! !

Raincatcher... Snowsnatcher

What to Use

- dishpan or other large, flat pan
- waterproof marker
- very narrow glass jar
- ruler

What to Do

1. Make a clear mark on the inside of the pan one inch from the bottom of the pan.

2. Set the pan outside on a day when it is raining or snowing heavily.

3. When the pan is filled to the one inch mark, bring it inside and immediately pour it into the narrow jar. Do this before the snow melts!

4. Very quickly, mark the level of the rain or snow on the outside of the jar with the marker. Then divide that distance into 10 even spaces, making a mark for each one. Label them 1/10 through 10/10 from bottom to top.

5. Now you have a gauge that will help you measure snow or rain, even in very small amounts.

6. Catch rain or snow in the large pan. At the end of the day, pour your catch into the rain/snow gauge for measuring. Remember that you must measure the snow before it melts. If you let the snow melt before measuring, then you will find out the amount of precipitation rather than the amount of snowfall.

266

Invitation to a Thunderstorm

What to Do

1. When you hear thunder, pay special attention. Watch the sky for lightning. If both lightning and thunder are present, use a watch to find out how much time passes between the lightning flash and the thunderclap.

2. Write down the amount of time. Each second between lightning and thunder represents approximately one mile of distance between you and the storm. How close is the storm??

3. Keep timing the intervals between lightning and thunder. Write down the distances. Is the storm moving closer or farther away?

4. Try writing down the time as well as the amount of distance between you and the storm. Can you figure out how fast the storm is moving??

What to Use

- stopwatch or clock
- pencil and paper
- thunderstorm

267

It's Raining, It's Pouring

The next time it rains on a warm day, DON'T STAY INSIDE!
Go outside and enjoy the rain!!

Build dams to collect or reroute water.
Float boats and leaves on the streams.
Remove the dams when you're through playing.

Put on your bathing suit and run, jump, splash, dance, and sing in the rain!

Sit on your porch and watch the rain. Close your eyes and listen to the sounds.

Before it rains, build a shelter. When the rain starts, go and sit under it so you can enjoy the smell of the rain and the feel of the wet air.

Collect rainwater and measure it. Or, use it to make mud pies and other pretend treats.

CAUTION: DO NOT GO IN THE RAIN IF IT'S LIGHTNING!

Rain, Rain, Don't Go Away!

What to Do

1. Put white drawing paper on top of the cardboard.

2. Paint a rainbow on the paper. Make bold, bright stripes.

3. Put your painted rainbow out in the rain. Lay it on the ground or sidewalk.

4. After a few minutes, bring your painting back inside and lay it flat on the floor to dry.

5. When the paper is dry, take it off the cardboard and mount it on construction paper or posterboard for showing off on your wall.

What to Use

- white drawing paper
- heavy cardboard
- rainbow colored poster paints
- paint brush
- colored construction paper or posterboard
- rainy day

Keep your own Weatherwatch for a month.
Compare your weather reports to those you
hear on the radio or TV or see in your local newspaper.

Weatherwatching

April

Date: 1

Time: afternoon
Sky looks: grey
Clouds: nimbus
Temperature: 42°
Precipitation: Wet, cold,
and miserable!

What to Use

- notebook
- markers
- pen or pencil
- clock
- calendar

What to Do

1. Make a Weather Log similar to this one.

2. Every day near the end of the day, write a description of the day's weather in your log. Do this every day for a month. Use your homemade weather vane, barometer and rain catcher to help you tell about the weather.

3. At the end of the month, look back over your log. What has the month's weather been like?

build a barometer

This is a tool that can help you predict the weather. A BAROMETER measures changes in air pressure. Usually a change in air pressure means that the weather is about to change. Falling pressure may mean a storm is on its way and rising pressure often signals clear weather ahead.

What to Use

- drinking straw
- large balloon
- glass jar
- strong rubber band
- glue
- cardboard strip
- pen
- scissors

HIGH —

LOW —

What to Do

1. Make your barometer on a clear day. Cut a circle from the balloon rubber large enough to fit over the top of the jar.

2. Stretch the rubber tightly over the jar and have someone help you fasten it with the rubber band.

3. Glue one end of the straw to the center of the rubber. Hold it in place until the glue dries.

4. Set the jar in a place where the temperature doesn't change a lot. Hang a piece of cardboard next to the jar so that it almost touches the free end of the straw.

5. Make a mark above the straw on the cardboard. Label it HIGH. Mark below the straw. Label it LOW.

6. Watch the straw over the next few days. The balloon will move up when air pressure outside the jar falls. This will cause the straw to dip down toward the LOW mark. When the pressure outside the jar rises, the balloon will move down and the straw will rise up toward the HIGH mark.

7. Use your barometer to make predictions about the coming weather. Compare your predictions with the weather forecast on the news.

Weathergrams

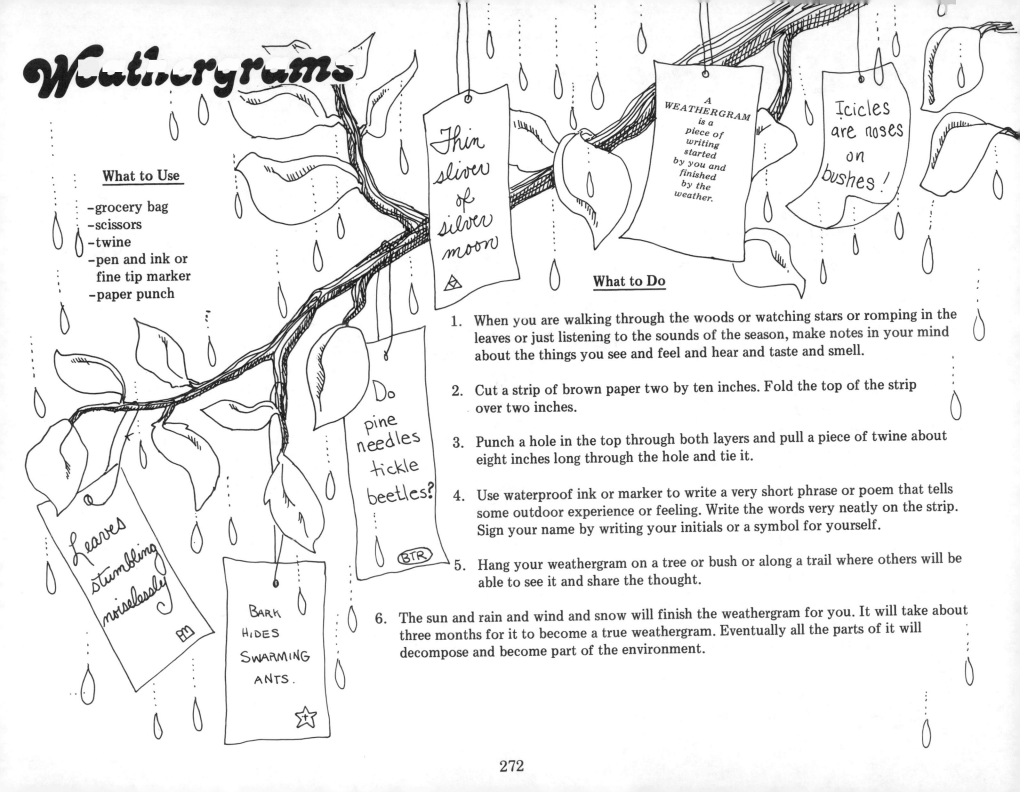

What to Use

- grocery bag
- scissors
- twine
- pen and ink or fine tip marker
- paper punch

Thin sliver of silver moon

A WEATHERGRAM is a piece of writing started by you and finished by the weather.

Icicles are noses on bushes!

Do pine needles tickle beetles? BTR

Leaves stumbling noiselessly

BARK HIDES SWARMING ANTS.

What to Do

1. When you are walking through the woods or watching stars or romping in the leaves or just listening to the sounds of the season, make notes in your mind about the things you see and feel and hear and taste and smell.

2. Cut a strip of brown paper two by ten inches. Fold the top of the strip over two inches.

3. Punch a hole in the top through both layers and pull a piece of twine about eight inches long through the hole and tie it.

4. Use waterproof ink or marker to write a very short phrase or poem that tells some outdoor experience or feeling. Write the words very neatly on the strip. Sign your name by writing your initials or a symbol for yourself.

5. Hang your weathergram on a tree or bush or along a trail where others will be able to see it and share the thought.

6. The sun and rain and wind and snow will finish the weathergram for you. It will take about three months for it to become a true weathergram. Eventually all the parts of it will decompose and become part of the environment.

Hurrah

For

City Sidewalks !

Sidewalk Games

YOUR SIDEWALK IS A GAMEBOARD

What to Do

1. Choose a stretch of sidewalk for your gameboard. Look for a sidewalk space that continues for more than 20 squares. It can even go around the whole block!

2. Use chalk to write directions or draw things on some of the spaces. This gameboard will give you ideas, but use your imagination to add directions of your own.

What to Use

- chalk
- dice or spinner
- sidewalk
- 2 or more players

3. Each player begins on START, tosses the dice or spins a spinner and then moves that number of spaces. Players must follow the directions of spaces they land on. You might want to make a rule that, if a player lands where another player is standing, the first player goes back to START!

FINISH

START

HAT

DOUBLE YOUR NEXT TOSS!

Dropped your hat! Go back to get it

ACE

STOP FOR ICE CREAM MISS 1 TURN

GAS STATION

SLIDE BACK 4 SPACES

Hey! This is fun to play alone! See how long it takes you to get to FINISH!

274

SIDEWALK WATER BALLOON DUEL

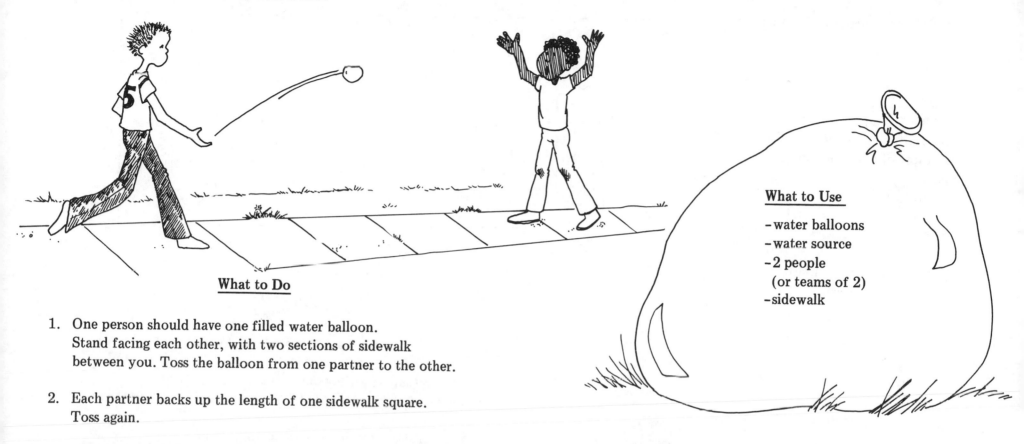

What to Do

What to Use

- water balloons
- water source
- 2 people
  (or teams of 2)
- sidewalk

1. One person should have one filled water balloon.
   Stand facing each other, with two sections of sidewalk
   between you. Toss the balloon from one partner to the other.

2. Each partner backs up the length of one sidewalk square.
   Toss again.

3. Keep moving apart and tossing until the balloon breaks. If you
   are not playing on a sidewalk, each take two giant steps
   backwards after each toss.

4. When the balloon breaks, count the number of sidewalk blocks
   between you. Try to beat that distance the next time you play.

5. THEN, try this: Stand back-to-back, each holding a water balloon.
   Have someone count 1-2-3-FIRE. As they count, you each take
   three giant steps, turn and throw the balloon. Each tries to catch
   the other balloon without breaking it.

275

SIDEWALK SHUFFLEBOARD

What to Use

- chalk
- 10 lids from jars
  (about the same size)
- 2 colors of construction
  paper
- scissors
- pencil
- glue
- 2 sticks
  (forked sticks work well)
- 2 players

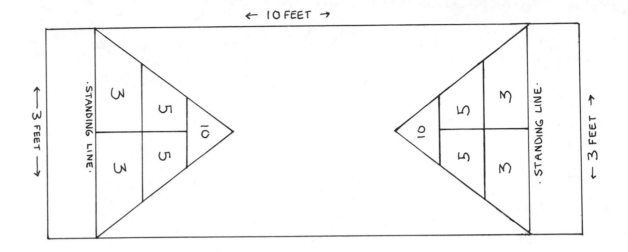

What to Do

1. Use chalk to draw a shuffleboard court similar to the one above on a sidewalk or driveway. Make it about 10 feet long and 3 feet wide. Be sure to write point values in each section. You can choose any point values you wish for the sections.

2. Make pucks for each player by gluing circles of one color onto five of the jar lids. Cut the circles from your construction paper. Choose a different color for each player.

3. You are ready to play. Player 1 starts at one end and uses his stick to shoot all five of his pucks towards the sections at the other end.

   Player 2 then shoots all five of her pucks from the other end.

   When both players have shot all their pucks, add up the scores by watching where the pucks are in their FINAL resting place. (Some of them may have been knocked around by other pucks.)

4. Play until one player has a score of 100 or more.

276

Draw a target on the sidewalk. Give each ring a point value. Draw a shooting line at least three feet away from the target. Using a shooter, each player shoots six marbles at the target. Keep track of your score and try to improve it on the next round.

Draw a hopscotch board on the sidewalk and play by your usual rules. ONLY . . all players must toss the stone backwards (lean over and throw between your legs) and hop backwards.

Draw a line about 8 inches from a wall. Draw another line six feet from the wall. Kneel or sit behind the farthest line. Toss 10 pennies. Try to get them behind the line close to the wall WITHOUT touching the wall. How many could you do that way? Try another 10 tosses. Can you improve your score?

With chalk, draw a two-foot square on the sidewalk or driveway. Divide it into four smaller squares. Number the small squares 1-2-3-4. Now, take turns jumping rope with two people turning for the jumper. Try to jump from square 1 to 2 to 3 to 4 without touching any chalk lines.

WHICH SIGN IS WHICH?

This is a game you can play using the signs that you'll find all over your neighborhood.

What to Use

- 20 index cards for each player
- 2 rubber bands for each player
- crayon or marker for each player
- large envelope for each player
- several players

What to Do

1. Get ready to play. Make sure each player has 20 cards, 2 rubber bands, a crayon or marker and an envelope.

2. Decide on a time limit for the sign search.

3. All the players go off to find 10 interesting signs. Look for signs without words or with few words.

4. For each sign, draw a picture on one card and write what the sign means on a second card. This will give each player 10 sign cards and 10 direction cards. Put a rubber band around each pile of 10 cards and put both piles into the envelope.

5. When the players get back together, they should trade envelopes. Then each player tries to properly match the signs with their meanings.

Sign Up!

GAS
☆
FOR LESS

NO PARKING IN DRIVEWAY

What to Use

- copy of this page
- pencil and notebook

Most neighborhoods are full of signs giving directions and information to people who live there or pass through. Get to know the signs in your neighborhood by going off on a sign scavenger hunt. Get your friends to join you!!

LIBRARY

PHONE

MIDDLETOWN
POPULATION 2817

DELI

What to Do

1. Copy the list on this sheet.

2. Set a time limit for yourself OR take as much time as you want.

3. Take the list, pencil and notebook and start reading your neighborhood's signs!

4. Compare your findings with your friends' lists.

SNOW EMERGENCY ROUTE

↑ UP

YIELD

SPEED LIMIT 55

← FOOD

SIGN UP!		
Find a sign that:	Picture of Sign	Location
Gives directions		
Warns		
Advertises		
Tells what to do		
Tells what not to do		
Has a one word direction		
Names a building		
Names a town		
Names a street or road		
Gives information		
Tells speed limit		
Gives location of something		
Is only for pedestrians		
Is only for trains		
Is only for cars		
Has to do with a school		
Has to do with children		
Has this shape ○		
Has this shape ⬡		
Has this shape △		
Has this shape ▭		
Has this shape ⬓		

View from a Sidewalk

Watch the world from your sidewalk and find out what really goes on outside your own front door!

What to Do

1. Find a comfortable place to sit for sidewalk-side watching. You might take a cushion or chair along if you're going to be there for awhile. Sit for a half hour or more. Keep notes in your notebooks. Make note of the date and time.

2. WATCH PEOPLE: *How many people walk by?*
   What ages are they?
   What kinds of looks are on their faces?
   Where do you think they're going?
   What do you think they're thinking?
   How many of the people do you know?
   How does the number of people walking compare to the numbers driving or riding buses or bicycles?
   Are there people working in the streets?
   Are there people out who aren't going anywhere?
   What are they doing?
   Are there any loiterers?

3. WATCH TRAFFIC: *How busy are the streets?*
   How much traffic is there? What kind of traffic?
   Count the cars, buses, skateboards, bicycles, etc.
   How full are the cars or trains or buses?

4. WATCH ANIMALS: *What different animals are out?*
   How many are alone? How many are with people?
   What are the animals doing?

5. WATCH HOUSES: *Are they close together? Far apart?*
   Are they alike? Different? Large? Small?
   What are the houses made of?
   Are there people coming out? Going in?

6. NOTICE: *From where you sit can you see anything . . .*

. . . funny?	*. . . messy?*	*. . . sad?*	*. . . dangerous?*
. . . broken?	*. . . green?*	*. . . joyful?*	*. . . expensive?*
. . . unusual?	*. . . frightening?*	*. . . neat?*	*. . . very old?*
. . . clean?	*. . . brand new?*	*. . . growing?*	*. . . mysterious?*

Visit Our Sidewalk Cafe

What to Use

- small table or large box for counter
- chairs (optional)
- ice chest or thermos jug
- paper cups and napkins
- posterboard and markers for signs
- drinks or other goodies to sell
- friends to help you
- containers for food

What to Do

1. Find a spot where you can set up your cafe. Choose an area where there are lots of people passing by and where your customers will have a place to sit and enjoy a snack.

2. Set up your counter and other furniture you may have gathered for the cafe.

3. Decide on your menu and prices. Try to sell items that can be made at low cost. You might consider sun tea, iced water, lemonade, watermelon chunks or graham crackers for summer and some warm teas for winter.

4. Prepare your food and put it in containers that will keep it cold (or warm) and fresh.

5. Set up, make your signs and menus and open the cafe when you're ready!

SAM AND SOPHIE'S
MENU
SUN Tea ..... 10¢
Natural Cookies ... 10¢
Ice WATER .... 5¢
Watermelon .... 15¢
Frozen CHERRIES ... 3 for 5¢

281

Often a neighborhood has more things and places than its people realize. Take time to take a tour of your neighborhood to learn just what treasures it has!

Neighborhood Treasures

NEIGHBORHOOD INVENTORY	
What we have:	How many:
play areas	
trash containers	
public phones	
churches	
fire hydrants	
fences	
bus stops	
broken down cars	
stop signs	
broken windows	
yards	
porches	
things being built	
newly painted buildings	
public benches	
parking lots	
fire escapes	
train stations	
jogging trails	
bicycle paths	

What to Use

-the NEIGHBORHOOD INVENTORY list
-pencil
-book to put underneath your paper

What to Do

1. Make a NEIGHBORHOOD INVENTORY list similar to this one. Leave some spaces for things you'll want to add to your list.

2. Take the list, a pencil and a book and go off on your investigating trip. This may take more than one trip, so plan to go as many times as you need to. Use the list to keep track of what you find.

3. When you're finished inventorying your neighborhood, look over the list to see how much stuff you've got right around your corner!

What do you think is great about your neighborhood?
What are your neighborhood's problems?
Wouldn't it be interesting to do this again in 10 years and see how things have changed?

Sidewalk Sound Search

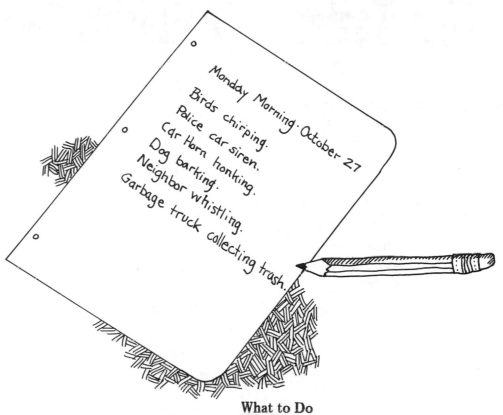

Monday Morning. October 27

Birds chirping.
Police car siren.
Car Horn honking.
Dog barking.
Neighbor whistling.
Garbage truck collecting trash.

What to Use

- paper and pencil
- tape recorder, if available

What to Do

1. Some day when you're out on the sidewalk, listen to the sounds of your neighborhood. Make a list of the sounds you hear. How many different ones can you find?

2. Listen on other days. Try listening early in the morning, in the middle of the day, in the late afternoon and at night. Listen for people sounds, traffic sounds, animal sounds, weather sounds.

3. If you have a tape recorder, try to capture some of the sounds on tape.

4. Listen for silence in your neighborhood. How often are there no sounds?

Air Tester... Pollution Catcher

What's in the air you breathe?
Find out by capturing some of that stuff
so you can get a close-up look!

What to Use

−clear glass dish or pie plate
−vaseline
−magnifying glass
−tweezers

What to Do

1. Smear vaseline all over the inside bottom of the dish.

2. Set the dish outside on a windowsill or porch. Leave it there for several days. (If it looks like rain, bring it inside.)

3. Examine your catch with the magnifying glass. Use tweezers to separate the larger particles so you can get a closer look at them.

284

Trash Can Beauty

Get a crew of kids to volunteer to turn the dull, dirty trash cans in your neighborhood into wonderful works of art!

What to Use

- metal trash cans
- enamel paint
- paint brushes
- turpentine
- plenty of newspapers
- detergent and water
- pencil and paper

What to Do

1. Wash and dry the trash can well.

2. See if you can round up some leftover enamel paints.

3. Plan your designs or pictures on paper. Let your imagination go! There are all kinds of ways to beautify a trash can.

4. Find a good spot outside for painting. Put down lots of newspaper around your painting area.

5. Gather painting supplies and get started. If the can is not too marked up, you can paint the designs directly onto the shiny surface. If it's pretty battered, you may need to cover the whole can with a background coat. Wait until this is very dry before you paint pictures on top of it.

6. When you're finished, clean up your paint and the brushes and any other messes.

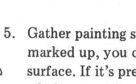

Talk to a Building

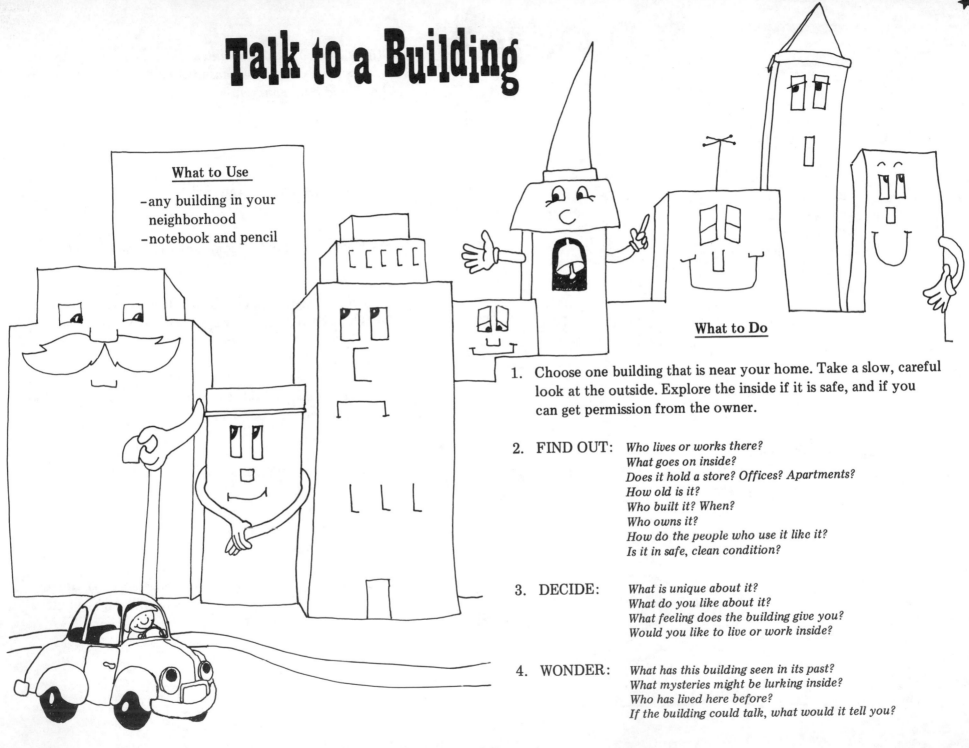

What to Use

- any building in your neighborhood
- notebook and pencil

What to Do

1. Choose one building that is near your home. Take a slow, careful look at the outside. Explore the inside if it is safe, and if you can get permission from the owner.

2. FIND OUT:
   Who lives or works there?
   What goes on inside?
   Does it hold a store? Offices? Apartments?
   How old is it?
   Who built it? When?
   Who owns it?
   How do the people who use it like it?
   Is it in safe, clean condition?

3. DECIDE:
   What is unique about it?
   What do you like about it?
   What feeling does the building give you?
   Would you like to live or work inside?

4. WONDER:
   What has this building seen in its past?
   What mysteries might be lurking inside?
   Who has lived here before?
   If the building could talk, what would it tell you?

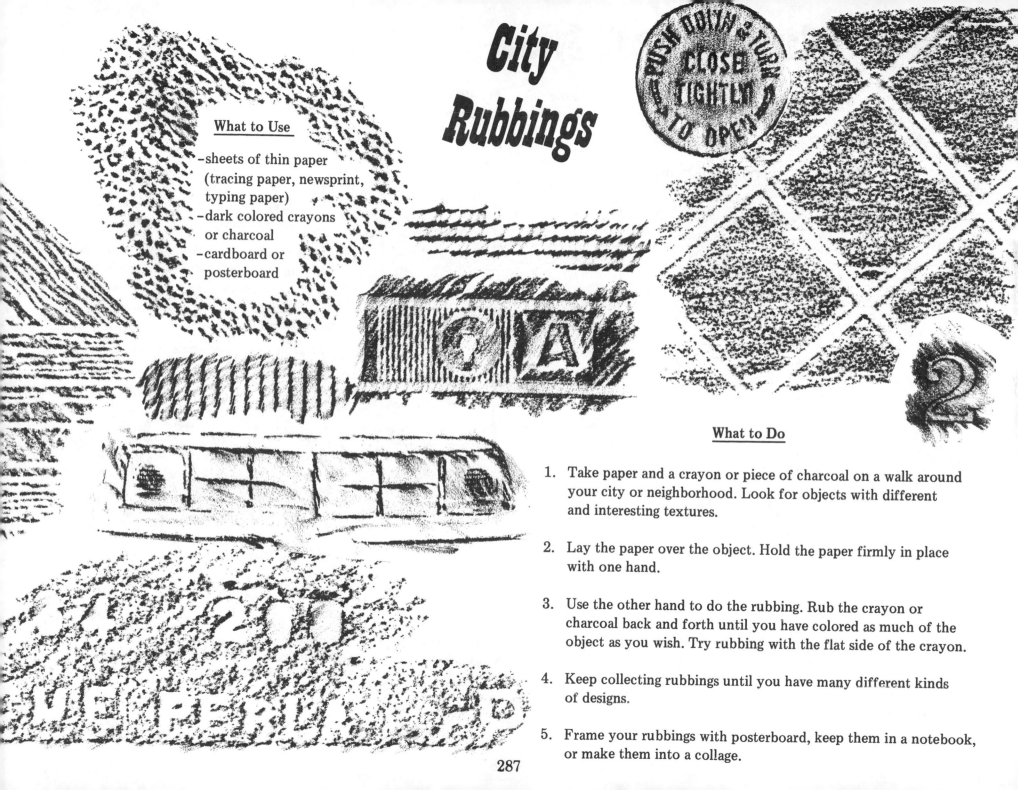

City Rubbings

What to Use

- sheets of thin paper (tracing paper, newsprint, typing paper)
- dark colored crayons or charcoal
- cardboard or posterboard

What to Do

1. Take paper and a crayon or piece of charcoal on a walk around your city or neighborhood. Look for objects with different and interesting textures.

2. Lay the paper over the object. Hold the paper firmly in place with one hand.

3. Use the other hand to do the rubbing. Rub the crayon or charcoal back and forth until you have colored as much of the object as you wish. Try rubbing with the flat side of the crayon.

4. Keep collecting rubbings until you have many different kinds of designs.

5. Frame your rubbings with posterboard, keep them in a notebook, or make them into a collage.

287

Gardens in Small Spaces

If you live in a place where there isn't much space for growing things, you don't have to go without a garden. There are some places that are just right for city gardening! You can grow things . . . .

. . . ON A WINDOWSILL

GARDENING TIPS:

Keep the soil moist, but don't flood your plants!

Prepare your planter by poking holes in the bottom of your containers to allow for drainage. It's also a good idea to put some gravel in the bottom of each container.

dill   parsley   mint   thyme   chives

HERBS . . . Plant seeds for dill, parsley, mint, thyme or chives in small containers of potting soil. When herbs are tall, snip some off, tie them in a bundle and hang them up to dry for several days. When they're dry, crumble the herbs and store them in a tight jar.

AVOCADOS . . . Wash avocado pits and use toothpicks to suspend them in a jar of water. Keep the water level about to the halfway point of the pit.

SWEET POTATOES . . . Choose potatoes that have some dark eyes on them. Suspend them in jars of water just as you did the avocados.

What to Use

- cottage cheese containers
- cut-off milk cartons
- styrofoam coffee cups
- flower pots
- coffee cans
- jars or glasses
- potting soil and gravel
- water
- plants or seeds or pits
- toothpicks

PINEAPPLE TOPS . . . Cut two-inch slices off the top of a pineapple. Remove all of the outer leaves. Dry out the slice for a day, then plant it in dirt. Keep the soil moist.

CARROT TOPS . . . Cut two-inch slices off the tops of carrots. Remove the outside leaves. Plant the carrot tops in tall milk cartons filled with soil.

BEET TOPS . . . Cut two-inch slices from the tops of beets. Plant the beet tops in soil.

...ON A PORCH OR ROOF OR PATIO

What to Use

- Containers:
    - dishpans
    - flowerpots
    - milk cartons
    - boxes
    - bushel baskets
    - pails
    - cans
    - trash cans
- lots of newspapers
- potting soil
- water
- gravel

- Seeds or seedlings:
    - herbs
    - small tomatoes
    - carrots
    - radishes
    - beets
    - leaf lettuce
    - lemons
    - squash
    - flowers
    - green houseplants
- hammer and nail
- waterproof paint and brush

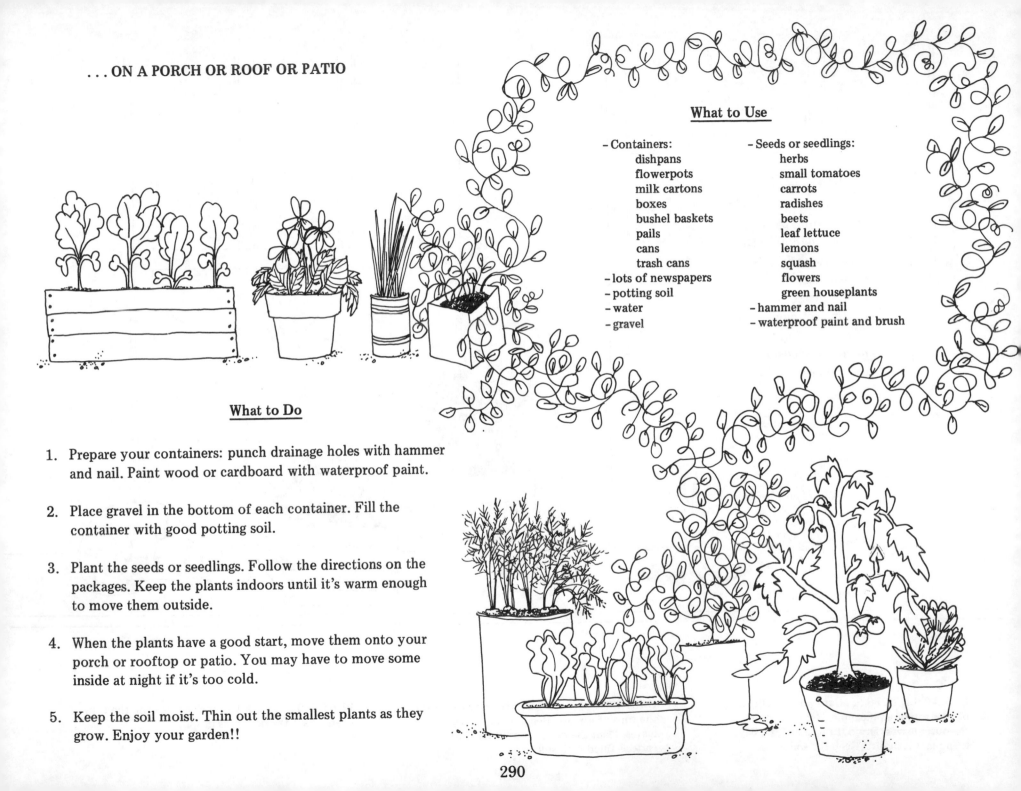

What to Do

1. Prepare your containers: punch drainage holes with hammer and nail. Paint wood or cardboard with waterproof paint.

2. Place gravel in the bottom of each container. Fill the container with good potting soil.

3. Plant the seeds or seedlings. Follow the directions on the packages. Keep the plants indoors until it's warm enough to move them outside.

4. When the plants have a good start, move them onto your porch or rooftop or patio. You may have to move some inside at night if it's too cold.

5. Keep the soil moist. Thin out the smallest plants as they grow. Enjoy your garden!!

290

... IN A SPONGE

What to Do

1. Soak the sponge in water for 10 minutes. Then squeeze out the water.

2. Drop seeds into some of the sponge's holes.

3. Tie the string around the sponge and hang it up where it will get plenty of sunshine.

4. Keep the sponge moist by gently watering it every day (more often, if necessary). You can spray the sponge or hold a dish of water up underneath it for a few minutes.

5. Watch your garden for about two weeks. When the plants are big enough, cut some off. The best part about this garden is that you can eat it on your sandwich!

What to Use

-round natural sponge (with plenty of holes)
-seeds (cress, mung beans, parsley or mustard seeds)
-string
-water
-spot with plenty of light

. . . IN A JUG

What to Do

1. Carefully wash and dry your jug.

2. Put the funnel in the jug and pour the gravel through it. One inch will be enough to provide proper drainage.

3. Pour in twice as much potting soil as gravel. Then add several small pieces of charcoal to keep the jug environment sweet-smelling.

4. Smooth the surface of the soil with the wooden stick.

5. Decide how you want to arrange the plants in the jug. Use the stick to make a hole for each plant's roots. Gently drop the plants in one at a time and use the stick to guide each to its spot. Then cover the roots with dirt.

6. When your plants are happily bedded, sprinkle them well with water and cork or cap the jug. Place your garden-in-a-jug in a bright indoor spot away from direct sunlight. If the inside of the jug collects a lot of drops of water, uncover it for a day or two.

What to Use

—wide-mouthed jug with a top (five-gallon pickle jars from restaurants are great!)
—funnel
—small plants
—charcoal pieces
—gravel
—potting soil
—long wooden stick
—soap and water

292

Track Down City Creatures

There are more wild creatures in cities and suburbs than you think. Be on the lookout for these and others.

What to Use

- list of creatures
- pencil
- book to rest paper on

What to Do

1. Keep your eyes open all the time for wild creatures. You might even go on a special hunt.

2. When you see an animal, write down where you saw it. DO NOT TOUCH OR PICK UP ANY WILD CREATURES. They may be harmful or carry germs.

3. Add any other animals to the list that you see running wild in your city.

CITY CREATURES TO FIND	
Animal	Where I Saw It
Ant	
Housefly	
Worm	
Termite	
Fruit Fly	
Cockroach	
Mouse	
Squirrel	
Rat	
Raccoon	
Pigeon	
Other Bird	
Other	

CREATE·A·CITY

Try out your skills as an architect or a city planner and create your own stone city.

What to Use

-stones, rocks, and pebbles
-liquid glue
-small mirrors
-twigs
-sand
-paints
-brushes
-large box top
-paper
-string
-scissors
-tape
-cellophane

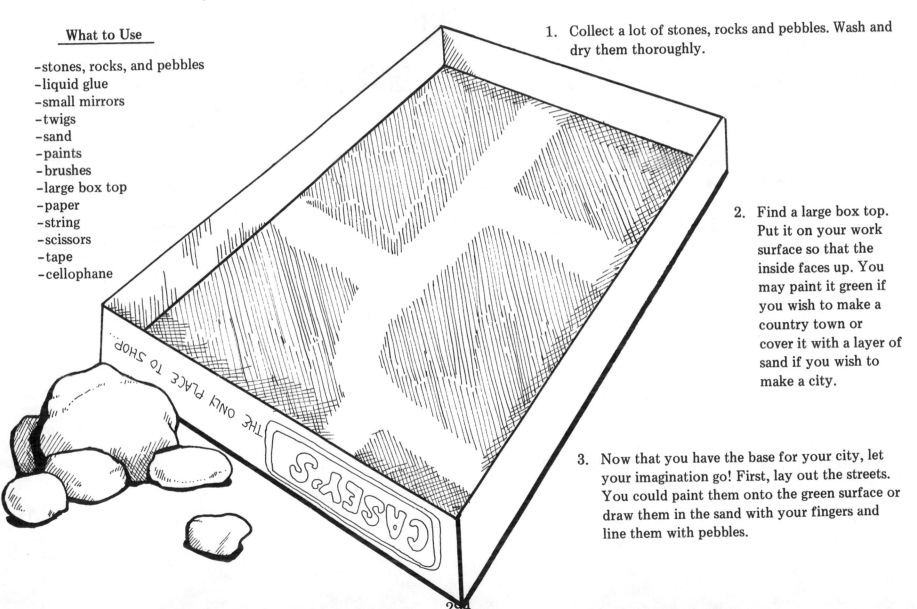

1. Collect a lot of stones, rocks and pebbles. Wash and dry them thoroughly.

2. Find a large box top. Put it on your work surface so that the inside faces up. You may paint it green if you wish to make a country town or cover it with a layer of sand if you wish to make a city.

3. Now that you have the base for your city, let your imagination go! First, lay out the streets. You could paint them onto the green surface or draw them in the sand with your fingers and line them with pebbles.

294

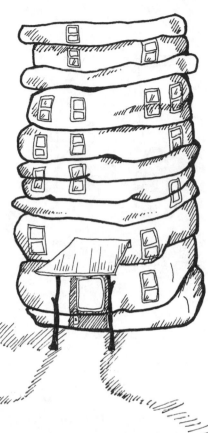

4. Next, start on the buildings. To make a skyscraper, choose several large, flat rocks. Stack these one on top of another and place some glue between each layer. After the glue dries, paint on windows, balconies, and doors. Find two small twigs and place these on either side of the entrance. Cut a small piece of paper and attach it to the twigs to make an awning. Don't forget to add stripes to it with your paints.

5. To make walls for houses, glue small stones on top of each other. Don't forget to leave holes for windows. When you have made four stacks, place them together, corner to corner, to form a square. Cut out a piece of paper and fold it in half to make a roof. Add detail to your roof by painting on shingles. Make a chimney by cutting out a square piece of paper, folding it into a cube, and taping it together. Cut the bottom to fit your roof and tape it in place. Paint it to look like bricks!

6. Your city needs stores, too. Build them just as you built houses, but leave the top half of the front open. Cut a piece of cellophane to fit and tape it into place. Then cut and fold a piece of paper for the roof. Be sure to add a sign out front so the inhabitants of your town will know what kind of store it is!

7. Every city should have a park and a playground to be used by healthy, happy citizens. Choose an area for your park, and put a small mirror there for a lake. Push some tall twigs into the sand around the mirror for trees (stick them in little globs of clay if you painted your box top), and make walking paths in the area the same way you made streets. You can make a swing set for your park. Find five twigs. Tie two together with string so they form a triangle, and do the same with two more. Push these into the sand so the tied ends are up. Now, lay the fifth twig across the tops. Tie one end of a short string around a pebble, then tie the other end around the crossbar, and you have a swing set!

8. You could make a see saw, too! Follow the directions for the swing set but use shorter twigs. Then find one long stick and lay it across the bar (see picture).

9. Remember that cities need green and growing things for the citizens to enjoy. Add lots of trees by pushing twigs into the sand or clay. Paint lots of little pebbles like flowers and shrubs, and put them around the houses and in the park. If you can find more mirrors, add them around the city to make more lakes and ponds. Put a welcome sign that tells the name of your city.

10. Now that your city is all built, it needs some people to live in it. See page 34 for instructions on making stone people.

Good Books To Know

FOR GROWNUPS TO USE WITH KIDS

Abruscato, Joe and Jack Hassard. LOVING AND BEYOND: SCIENCE TEACHING FOR THE HUMANISTIC CLASSROOM. Goodyear, 1976.

Science is a human experience. That is the premise of this book that teaches teachers how to be more effective in introducing their students to the many science activities included.

Cornell, Joseph Bharat. SHARING NATURE WITH CHILDREN. Ananda, 1979.

A book of games for grownups to share with children to instruct and inspire them in the ways of nature. The description of each game includes the concepts, attitudes, and qualities it teaches as well as when, where, and how to play it.

DeVito, Alfred and Gerald H. Krockover. CREATIVE SCIENCING. Little, Brown, & Co., 1976.

A book mostly for teachers about developing science skills in their students. Experiments are designed to develop skills in observation, classification, interpretation, and more in the areas of biology, chemistry, environmental science, and physics.

Nickelsburg, Janet. NATURE ACTIVITIES FOR EARLY CHILDHOOD. Addison-Wesley, 1976.

This book, written by an eighty-four year old science teacher, teaches children the art of observation. It is also full of interesting tidbits about the creatures being observed.

Russell, Helen Ross. TEN-MINUTE FIELD TRIPS. J.G. Ferguson Publishing Co., 1973.

An elementary school teacher's guide for using the school grounds—any school grounds, whether concrete, grass, or sand—for environmental studies.

Skelsey, Alice and Gloria Huckaby. GROWING UP GREEN: PARENTS AND CHILDREN GARDENING TOGETHER. Workman, 1973.

A celebration of growing things for children and their parents. This book advocates a lifestyle of growing green things and children and thus discovering the goodness of the earth. "Greenthink" is the key.

Strongin, Herb. SCIENCE ON A SHOESTRING. Addison-Wesley, 1976.

Loads of 30–60 minute scientific investigations—all of them very low cost!

IDEAS FOR ARTS AND CRAFTS WITH NATURAL MATERIALS

Cole, Ann, Carolyn Haas, Elizabeth Heller and Betty Weinberger. A PUMPKIN IN A PEAR TREE. Little, Brown & Co., 1976.

Simple-to-make holiday arts and crafts projects using easily available materials and fun, creative ideas.

Cutler, Katherine N. CREATIVE SHELLCRAFT. Lothrop, Lee & Shepard Co., 1971.

Clearly-written suggestions for finding, cleaning, storing, and using sea shells in a variety of creative ways.

Cutler, Katherine N. FROM PETALS TO PINECONES. Lothrop, Lee & Shepard, 1969.

A guidebook for nature craft projects which gives clear directions and ideas for all sorts of creative gifts and decorations. Stresses conservation and the development of the "seeing eye" so that children can learn to see creative possibilities in natural objects.

Fiarotta, Phyllis. SNIPS AND SNAILS AND WALNUT WHALES. Workman Publishing Co., 1975.

Over 100 nature craft projects for children with step-by-step instructions and illustrations that show how to make crafts from natural materials.

Gjersvik, Maryanne. GREEN FUN. The Chatam Press, Inc., 1974.

Instant toys, tricks, and amusements to make from common weeds, seeds, leaves, and flowering things.

Graham, Ada. FOXTAILS, FERNS, AND FISH SCALES: A HANDBOOK OF ART AND NATURE PROJECTS. Four Winds Press, 1976.

An idea-filled book to teach the reader about natural materials and how to use them in making inexpensive arts and crafts creations.

Hawkinson, John. MORE TO COLLECT AND PAINT FROM NATURE. Albert Whitman & Co., 1964.

A book that gives simple instructions for observing and painting insects, birds, and animals.

Leeming, Joseph. HOLIDAY CRAFT AND FUN. J. B. Lippincott, 1950.

A book of easy-to-make party craft ideas for holidays, including invitations, favors, decorations, centerpieces, party hats, costumes, and games, which can easily be constructed at home.

MacConomy, Alma D., ed. WILDLIFE'S HOLIDAY ALBUM. National Wildlife Federation, 1978.

Beautiful photographs mixed with fascinating text filled with stories, poems, and interesting facts, plus many craft activities and delicious recipes make this book a delight to own and use.

O'Neill, Jeanne Lamb. THE MAKE-IT-MERRY CHRISTMAS BOOK. William Morrow & Company, Inc., 1977.

Simple, inexpensive ways to make 21 elegant gifts and decorations using treasures from nature, some household items, and lots of love.

Pettit, Florence H. HOW TO MAKE WHIRLIGIGS AND WHIMMY DIDDLES AND OTHER AMERICAN FOLKCRAFT OBJECTS. Thomas Y. Crowell Co., 1972.

Authoritative and detailed instructions for making more than 20 uniquely American folkcraft objects.

Product Development International Holding, N. V. THE FAMILY CREATIVE WORKSHOP, VOL. 2. Plenary Publications International, Inc., 1974.

All kinds of projects involving beachcombing, beads, beanbags, belts, birds, birthdays, bottles, and bicycles, with explicit directions, illustrations, and photographs.

Search Press Limited. THE BEAUTIFUL NATURECRAFT BOOK. Sterling Publishing Co., Inc., 1979.

Directions and beautiful full-color illustrations for making unusual crafts from simple, easy-to-find natural materials which you can collect without damaging the environment.

Search Press Limited. THE CHRISTMAS CRAFTS BOOK. Sterling Publishing Co., Inc., 1979.

Beautiful color photographs and explicit directions for making Christmas gifts, cards, candles, ornaments, etc., with natural materials and your own creativity and imagination.

Stribling, Mary Lou. ART FROM FOUND MATERIALS DISCARDED AND NATURAL. Crown Publishers, Inc., 1970.

A collection of art projects and technical guides (with illustrations and instructions) that opens the reader's eye to new and different ways of looking at and using discarded and natural materials.

SCIENCE, ECOLOGY AND GARDENING ACTIVITIES

Abruscato, Joe and Jack Hassard. THE EARTHPEOPLE ACTIVITY BOOK: PEOPLES, PLACES, PLEASURES AND OTHER DELIGHTS. Goodyear, 1978.

A look at the fascinating Earthpeople and their Peopledoings. Topics such as the earth's history, animal behavior, tricks our brains play on us, yummy things we love to eat, and things we like to do are included.

Abruscato, Joe and Jack Hassard. THE WHOLE COSMOS CATALOG OF SCIENCE ACTIVITIES. Goodyear, 1977.

More than a book of science experiments and activities—this is a book of awe, wonder, and the delight of discovery. It tells stories and introduces some people who have done great things in the world of science.

Allison, Linda. THE REASON FOR SEASONS. Little, Brown, & Co., 1975.

A book that is about seasons plus a whole lot more. Things to do, make, watch for, and collect during each or every season.

Allison, Linda. THE SIERRA CLUB SUMMER BOOK. Charles Scribner's Sons, 1977.

This book begins by explaining what summer is and why it is, then proceeds to give dozens of wonderful suggestions of what to do on summer days.

Jobb, Jamie. THE NIGHT SKY: AN EVERYDAY GUIDE TO EVERY NIGHT. Little, Brown, & Co., 1977.

A book for children to help discover nighttime skies and all the fascinating things they hold. It includes history, folklore, and lots of star maps and quizzes.

Kains, M. G. GARDENING FOR YOUNG PEOPLE. Stein and Day, 1978.

Deals with all aspects of gardening. A thorough and entertaining book full of anecdotes and written for children.

Kohn, Bernice. THE ORGANIC LIVING BOOK. Viking, 1972.

> *A beginning book about the hows and whys of loving the earth. It deals with conservation, pollution control, and ecology by teaching about yogurt, bugs, and gardens.*

Laurel, Alicia Bay. LIVING ON THE EARTH. Random House, 1970.

> *A sensitive book that discusses the simple life from backpacking to housing, furnishings, crafts, agriculture, food preparation, and more.*

Leverich, Kathleen and the Editors of *Cricket Magazine*. CRICKET'S EXPEDITIONS. Random House, 1977.

> *An explorer's guide for kids that helps them plan, prepare for, take, and relive expeditions to their neighborhood parks, schools, and around their homes.*

Miles, Betty. SAVE THE EARTH! AN ECOLOGY HANDBOOK FOR KIDS. Alfred A. Knopf, 1974.

> *A demonstration of how everything connects to everything else. Chapters on land, air, and water include poetry, real life examples of people taking action to save the earth, and projects that teach conservation. Ends with a how-to-do-it section for getting actively involved in the ecology movement.*

Newcomb, Duane. THE POSTAGE STAMP GARDEN BOOK. J. P. Tarcher, Inc., 1975.

> *A book for the home/backyard gardener that combines and modifies the French Intensive and organic methods, and promises success even to people with brown thumbs!*

Petrich, Patricia and Rosemary Dalton. THE KIDS' GARDEN BOOK. Nitty Gritty, 1974.

> *All about tools, light, terms, containers, soil, and rules for growing gardens in simple language and diagrams. Also includes instructions for the planting and caring of indoor gardens.*

Rey, H. A. FIND THE CONSTELLATIONS. Houghton Mifflin Co., 1976.

> *A scientifically accurate book for children that illustrates and explains the constellations. The book includes stories, quizzes, sky charts, time tables, and other helps to make learning easier and more fun.*

Rey, H. A. THE STARS: A NEW WAY TO SEE THEM. Houghton-Mifflin Co., 1976.

> *A practical, scientific book aimed at children but great for adults, too. Thorough, simple, and lively.*

Richards, Kay. SCIENCE MAGIC WITH PHYSICS. Arco, 1974.

> *Over one hundred harmless scientific experiments using inexpensive or household materials. Scientific theories behind the experiments are explained in simple terms.*

Rights, Mollie. BEASTLY NEIGHBORS. Little, Brown, & Co., 1981.

> *A book about the world kids live in, whether it be city, country, or rambling suburban estate. Lots of interesting projects and experiments are included.*

Simons, Robin. RECYCLOPEDIA. Houghton Mifflin, 1976.

> *All the projects in here are based on the recycling philosophy. Tells kids how to recycle and gives such ideas as how to make a popsicle stick thumb piano, a mayonnaise jar and tin can water clock, and a puzzle made of sponges.*

Simon, Seymour. PETS IN A JAR: COLLECTING AND CARING FOR SMALL WILD ANIMALS. Puffin Books, 1975.

> *This book will help young would-be naturalists observe and enjoy the wildness of animals. It provides instruction on the care and feeding of wild critters from tadpoles to starfish.*

Zim, Herbert S., and Robert H. Baker. STARS. Golden Press, 1951.

> *This book deals not just with stars, but with aspects of the whole sky. It is full of good illustrations as well as texts and written so that older children will easily understand it.*

GAMES AND EXERCISES AND GOOD INFORMATION ABOUT PHYSICAL FITNESS

Bershad, Carol and Deborah Bernick. BODYWORKS: THE KIDS' GUIDE TO FOOD AND PHYSICAL FITNESS. Random House, 1979.

> *A lively and extensive explanation of how bodies work. Fascinating tidbits of information and delightful illustrations make this book fun and practical for anyone.*

Carr, Rachel. CREATIVE YOGA EXERCISES FOR CHILDREN: BE A FROG, A BIRD, OR A TREE. Harper and Row, 1973.

> *Yoga is a good way to make young bodies strong and supple. This book tells kids how to do simple yoga exercises.*

Carr, Rachel. YOGA FOR ALL AGES. Simon and Schuster, 1972.

> *A beginning book of yoga adapted for the Western lifestyle. It includes a special chapter of yoga for children.*

Diskin, Eve. YOGA FOR CHILDREN. Warner, 1976.

A book of yoga exercises written to children with the idea of equipping them with a sense of fun and well-being.

Ferretti, Fred. THE GREAT AMERICAN BOOK OF SIDEWALK, STOOP, DIRT, CURB, AND ALLEY GAMES. Workman, 1975.

A revival of the old-time games city kids can still play with just the barest of necessities and a block's worth of kids.

Ferretti, Fred. THE GREAT AMERICAN MARBLE BOOK. Workman, 1973.

This is a little book full of the wonders and excitement of marble playing. It includes a history of marble playing, and a host of popular game rules.

Fluegelman, Andrew, ed. THE NEW GAMES BOOK. Doubleday, 1976.

Non-competitive games for people of all ages and groups of all sizes. This book is written in the spirit of spending a beautiful day celebrating laughter.

Haney, Erene Cheki and Ruth Richards. YOGA FOR CHILDREN. Bobbs–Merrill, 1973.

An easy-to-follow manual with instructive pictures for children to enjoy. The exercises are designed to keep young bodies flexible and active minds relaxed.

Orlick, Terry. THE COOPERATIVE SPORTS & GAMES BOOK: CHALLENGE WITHOUT COMPETITION. Pantheon Books, 1978.

An excellent book of games without losers, fit for all ages. The games are more than fun—they are vehicles of cooperation and sharing.

Schneider, Tom. EVERYBODY'S A WINNER. Little, Brown, & Co., 1976.

Everybody's a winner in this book because winning is defined as feeling good about ourselves through games that are fun for everyone, fitness programs that make the most of what we have, and appreciating the unique person each of us is.

Skolnik, Peter L. JUMP ROPE. Workman, 1974.

A book devoted to the ancient and universal art of jumping rope. It includes sections on the history, language, games, and rhymes for skipping rope.

Wilt, Joy. KEEPING YOUR BODY ALIVE & WELL. Word, Inc., 1976.

A book for young children that tells them what their basic physical needs are and how those needs may be met.

STILL MORE THINGS TO DO AND MAKE AND EAT

Baxter, Kathleen M. COME AND GET IT. A/A Printing, 1978.

A natural foods cookbook for children. The recipes are organized into four different grades from just starting through advanced.

Caney, Steven. PLAY BOOK. Workman, 1975.

A book full of imaginative and creative ways to play and things to make—indoors and outdoors.

Cooper, Jane. LOVE AT FIRST BITE. Alfred A. Knopf, 1977.

Recipes for lots of healthy, yummy things to make and eat. The format is simple and lots of fun and written so that kids can do most of the cooking without adult supervision.

Gray, Magda and Yvonne Deutsch. 215 IDEAS TO KEEP CHILDREN HAPPY: RAINY DAY PASTTIMES. London: Marshall Cavendish Pub. Ltd., 1975.

Marvelous games, ideas for gardening and cooking, and lots of things to make using household items to keep children amused. The instructions are easy to follow; the pictures and illustrations are beautiful.

Haas, Carolyn Buhai. THE BIG BOOK OF RECIPES FOR FUN. cbh, 1980.

A big book loaded with activities for kids from pre-school through sixth grade. Includes activities for use at home and school, indoors and outdoors.

Lane, Jane and John. HOW TO MAKE PLAY PLACES AND SECRET HIDY HOLES. Doubleday, 1979.

An instruction manual for the family showing step-by-step all the neat things that can be made with cardboard boxes.

McCoy, Elin. THE INCREDIBLE YEAR–ROUND PLAYBOOK. Random House, 1979.

Fun things to do and games to play with sun, sand, water, wind, and snow. Readable text and attractive illustrations.

Parents' Nursery School. KIDS ARE NATURAL COOKS. Houghton Mifflin, 1974.

> Good recipes and lively illustrations are presented to kids and for kids. Recipes, which make use of natural foods, are organized by seasons to make use of the fresh food available.

Stein, Sara Bonnett. THE KIDS' KITCHEN TAKEOVER. Workman, 1975.

> Kids aged five to twelve can use the kitchen for all kinds of things— making crafts, growing plants, observing the outside inside. And, of course, for cooking and baking good things to eat.

Vance, Eleanor Graham. THE EVERYTHING BOOK. Western Publishing Co., Inc., 1974.

> A sampler of things that children enjoy—everything from games and easily-made crafts and finger plays to a whole chapter devoted to the wonderful things that grandparents can do with kids.

Wiseman, Ann. MAKING THINGS: A HANDBOOK OF CREATIVE DISCOVERY. Little, Brown, and Co., 1975.

> This is a book that deals with philosophy as well as the making of interesting things from fishing nets to donut blouses to moccasins.

Index